Saving
the Great
Stone Face

Saving the Great Stone Face

the chronicle of the Old Man of the Mountain

by

Frances Ann Johnson Hancock

Edited by

Ruth Ayres-Givens

Published for the

FRANCONIA AREA HERITAGE COUNCIL

by

PHOENIX PUBLISHING

Canaan, New Hampshire

P E R M I S S I O N S

The many passages taken from the Littleton Courier *are reprinted with the kind permission of the publisher.*

The passages on pages 112-113 and 114-115 are reprinted with the kind permission of The Union Leader.

Excerpts from the article "Right Through Franconia Notch (at 70 m.p.h.)" on page 145 is reprinted with the kind permission of Yankee *Publishing,* Yankee Magazine, *and* Don Guy, *the author.*

The passages on pages 150-151 are reprinted with the kind permission of the Society for the Protection of New Hampshire Forests.

The excerpts which appear on pages 147 and 153 are reprinted with the kind permission of the New Hampshire Times.

The poem, "The Old Man of the Mountain" which appears on pages 16 and 160, is reprinted with the kind permission of the First Church of Christ, Scientist.

Hancock, Frances Ann Johnson, d. 1980.
    Saving the Great Stone Face.

  Bibliography: p. 172
  Includes index.
    1. Old Man of the Mountain (N.H.). I. Ayres-Givens,
  Ruth. II. Franconia Area Heritage Council. III. Title.
  F41.6.P9H36   1983   974.2'3   83-22961
  ISBN 0-914659-02-2

Printed in the United States of America
by Courier Printing Company.
Binding by New Hampshire Bindery
Design by A. L. Morris

This book

is dedicated to the memory

of our talented and spirited friend

Frances Ann Johnson Hancock

CONTENTS

FOREWORD

FRANCES ANN Johnson Hancock the author of this book, was a distinguished and prominent citizen of the New England North Country. She lived her life in proximity to Franconia Notch, was an author of prose and poetry as well as a composer. She was a devotee of the Old Man of the Mountain and on many occasions contributed to celebrations in his honor and to programs to help save him and Franconia Notch.

She was asked by Bernard Herbert, then Executive Director of the Franconia-Sugar Hill-Easton Chamber of Commerce, to write this book which had been envisaged as a project by a committee of the chamber. She was delighted to take on this task, agreeing that the proceeds should go to the Franconia History-Museum Committee.

Bernard Herbert decided to establish a special committee for review and publication of the book which included the names of a large number of prominent citizens who were deeply aware of the place of the Old Man in the history and life of the North Country.

When the first draft of the manuscript was completed a meeting with the author was held to discuss the book's publication. It was a matter of deep regret for all concerned that shortly thereafter the enthusiastic author, Frances Ann, was taken ill and died.

Bernard Herbert discussed with her family what should be done about the book and they unanimously agreed that they would hope that the committee, which he had established, would arrange for its editing and publication, and that the proceeds would go to the History-Museum Committee. The family also donated some of her important materials to this committee. The members of her family showed great public spirit and generosity which was and will continue to be deeply appreciated.

When Bernard Herbert had to leave Franconia at an unexpectedly early date, he asked me to try to carry on the work in his absence, as acting chairman of the Book Committee. With great insight and devotion, he had brought together an enthusiastic and effective working group and had arranged with Phoenix Publishing to publish the book.

Members of the committee who had knowledge of special areas of the book were asked to help where appropriate. Niels Nielsen contributed the chapter explaining the daring and effective work which he had done to save the profile from the devastation of northern New England weather. With the aid of Mary Taylor Fowler, I worked on the chapters dealing with public action to ensure the preservation of the Notch. Others on the committee contributed time and effort on various parts of the text. It was discovered that many of Frances Ann's quotations were imprecise in transcription, although never at variance with the thoughts expressed and many have been left as she gave them.

The Book Committee is especially grateful to Governor Sherman Adams who contributed the prologue, Paul Bofinger, President/Forester of the Society for the Protection of New Hampshire Forests, who wrote the epilogue, and Walter W. Wright, retired chief of Special Collections, Dartmouth College Library, who reviewed the manuscript and the bibliography and made numerous valuable suggestions. Phoenix Publishing has been of enormous help in bringing this book to reality. Thus, all of us have become partners in the great tradition of saving the Old Man, and bringing to public attention the extraordinary efforts required of thousands of people. We all have looked upon the prolongation of his life and his availability for public viewing within a wilderness environment as a sacred trust.

Ruth W. Ayres-Givens

Franconia, New Hampshire
July 15, 1983

INTRODUCTION

THE WORLD-FAMOUS natural wonder, the Great Stone Face, is known locally with special affection and pride as the Old Man or the Profile. For untold centuries he has gazed with serene dignity from his high cliffs on Profile Mountain near the upper gateway of Franconia Notch in the White Mountains of northern New Hampshire.

Survival has not been easy.

The Old Man, in his exposed location, has been and still is in constant danger of being destroyed. His safety has been threatened through the long centuries during and following his creation, especially in the comparatively brief span of time since he was discovered by Luke Brooks in 1805. Yet, miraculously, the Great Stone Face endures, in spite of the ever remodeling forces of nature and the wanton self-interests of man.

The latest crisis has been the recent controversy over whether "to build or not to build" a superhighway through the narrow defile of Franconia Notch. The upsetting possibility has once more alerted the Old Man's friends to the ever lurking presence of danger.

This book is intended as a timely review of the Old Man's dramatic history and as an urgent reminder of the need for our constant and determined guardianship of New Hampshire's foremost (and vulnerable) natural attraction and its beautiful surroundings.

Thus far the Old Man's survival has been made possible by the efforts of thousands of loyal admirers. They live not only in the near-by communities of Franconia, Easton, and Sugar Hill but also in neighboring towns, as well as throughout our state and nation, and even in many distant countries. Thanks to their devotion the Old Man still endures as one of the great natural wonders of the world.

In earlier times of crisis, when the Old Man's neighborhood and even his own existence have been threatened, people who cared have rallied to protect and preserve the granite Profile that is New Hampshire's official emblem and the impressive centerpiece of Franconia Notch, dedicated in 1928 as a beautiful memorial park. We must continue, always, to care!

Lamentably, we realize that nature itself gradually rearranges and alters everything it builds. Change is continual in our great out-of-doors; and so it is with our Old Man in Franconia Notch.

Frances Ann Johnson Hancock

Saving the Great Stone Face

Prologue

YEARS HENCE when the forces of nature finally triumph over the efforts of man to preserve the structure of the Great Stone Face, historians will be able to rely on the descriptive documentation that this volume provides of the narrative of events surrounding the efforts of state government and a handful of dedicated citizens who individually and collectively used every device then known to preserve the rocky conglomerate that miraculously forms the Profile protruding from the shoulder of Cannon Mountain. While a good deal is known about the origins and early history of New Hampshire, authors have been few and inadequate who have looked back upon significant events, often of local interest, that have had a marked effect upon the image and characteristics of this state. Stirring the public conscience to acquire and preserve Franconia Notch provided the impetus that changed the state seal and reidentified the image of New Hampshire, reasserting its individuality and restating its pride in its enormously beautiful natural assets.

Much copy has been written about the Great Stone Face, but, stripped of the poetry, fable and conjecture, the facts of much of its history have been uncoordinated fragments waiting to be put into chronological order comprehensible to the reader and the scholar searching for the composite whole of the history of the Notch.

The author has fortunately accepted the most plausible of the stories of the discovery of the Great Stone Face. Luke Brooks' outburst at the

1

shore of the Profile Lake in 1805 is a convincing episode of this history.

As the title of this history graphically suggests, this volume describes the efforts that so far have preserved the Profile as we know it today. Essentially the work has been done by individuals and not by government, either state or local. As the author accurately points out, the existence today of the Old Man is attributable to the efforts of three men, namely, Colonel Charles Greenleaf, the owner of the Profile House and the rocky cliffs which form the Profile itself; the Reverend Guy Roberts of Whitefield, who took it upon himself to find a way to prevent the further slippage of rock which formed the forehead of the Old Man; and Quarryman Edward H. Geddes of Quincy, Massachusetts, whose remarkable knowledge and ingenuity provided the means by which hinges, rods, and turnbuckles have so far prevented any significant slippage or further deterioration in the configuration of the Profile itself.

Although the author included in her text copious quotations taken from engineering studies and pertinent evidence offered for assistance, they clarify for the reader the series of events which overcame obstacles first thought insoluble. The Division of Parks, in whose custody the operation of Franconia Notch State Park now lies, has taken such measures to assure at least the temporary safety of the Old Man. This and other responsible state agencies have been joined by citizens' groups which have assumed the responsibility of monitoring the effects of time and the elements upon the work of nature. All concerned are well aware that vigilance is the price of safety, as it was of liberty over two hundred years ago.

Hancock gives considerable attention to the problem of settling the diverse points of view concerning the construction of a highway through the Notch suitable to meet the growing public demand for a travelable highway through some thirteen miles of narrow, treacherous terrain.

Since the planners who designed the interstate system of federal highways chose Franconia Notch as a principal north-south route between Concord and St. Johnsbury, Vermont, attention was quickly drawn to the effect of the construction of a four lane divided highway through the heart of Franconia Notch. Engineers and landscape architects quickly raised unanswerable questions about the effect of deep bed rock blasting upon the friable rock structure of the Profile cliffs, particularly the delicate balance of the supporting boulders beneath the rocks forming the features of the face of the Old Man. In broader perspective it became increasingly difficult for those predominantly concerned with aesthetic and environmental effects to accept the federal specifications that govern the construction of a road built in accordance with interstate standards. The author has followed the chain of events leading to a resolution of the issue with sufficient documentation and descriptive discourse to enable the reader to understand the logic of the agreement providing a compromise which the principal parties concerned could accept.

The reader must reserve judgment of the success of these negotiations until construction plans and layouts are sufficiently clear to enable the people who have been immersed in these discussions to make judgment as the work proceeds. Certainly the author has pulled together the arguments and considerations that will further promote understanding of the events that have surrounded an episode in the history of New Hampshire which has had national repercussions. To preserve the features of the Great Stone Face will demand a continuing public interest and the vigilance of the state custodians to whom are entrusted the administration of this public asset. Frances Hancock and the editor of this volume have earned the gratitude of the people of New Hampshire and of hosts of people everywhere whose interest in this natural phenomenon will remain of ongoing concern.

Sherman Adams

Prologue

The Old Man of the Mountain, Franconia Notch, New Hampshire
David Johnson, 1876
60" x 48"
Oil on canvas
Collection: State of New Hampshire

I

Origins

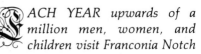ACH YEAR upwards of a million men, women, and children visit Franconia Notch and gaze up in wonder at the Old Man of the Mountain. Who knows how many millions in the past have paid their respects to this venerable Profile since his discovery over 175 years ago? It is probable that few of these millions of visitors ever thought that either the Old Man or the beauty of the wilderness Notch itself might be endangered by nature — or by the actions of men.

It is fairly certain that for the first half century following his discovery all who saw the Old Man considered him as permanent as the nearby rocky peaks of the Franconia Range. Those who saw the Profile in this first half century, from the surveyors who discovered him to Nathaniel Hawthorne, were filled with awe at the wondrous character of the face. First lean horses and then swift stagecoaches brought increasing numbers of tourists to stay at the inns and taverns. Doubtless many of these visitors expected to see landscapes as depicted by the early romantic White Mountain artists who looked upon the region as an arcadia and painted the mountains as they might wish to see them — with the ruggedness of the opening West.

As news and pictures of this paradise spread, New Hampshire's mountains opened up, not only to tourists, but also to the lumber interests which needed accessible forests to feed the Industrial Revolution's growing demand for wood.

But we are ahead of our story. In this first part, let us turn back to a time when the deep forests, sparkling streams, and great mountains stood as they had for thousands of years.

1

BACKGROUND HIGHLIGHTS

THE OLD MAN OF THE MOUNTAIN is a rock profile which juts out abruptly against the sky with unique grandure 1,200 feet above Profile Lake.

Geologists who have studied the formations of the area tell us that the Profile was formed partly by the shifting motions of the great American ice sheet as it moved over our White Mountains centuries ago and partly by the action of seasonal frost and ice in rock crevices. Together, the glacier and the weather gradually arranged certain rocks and ledges into a profile-forming position on the south shoulder of Profile Mountain.

Niels F. Nielsen, Jr., a construction engineer, who knows more, at first hand, than anyone else about the Profile, expresses this history thus: "The first citizen to reside in New Hampshire arrived between 10,000 and 25,000 years ago, when the ice sheet covering the area receded. It was then that the Old Man of the Mountain was born. The granite crystallized and some of the cliff fell away. Since then continuous freeze-thaw cycles combined with high winds and rain continue their destructive work, while dedicated men continue to labor to preserve the Profile from the destruction of time and the elements."

Stone experts have reported that the Profile is formed of friable granite, subject to gradual decomposition by the changing weather conditions of our North Country. It is cause for wonder and gratitude that the exposed profile-forming ledges have endured so long. How fortunate that deterioration has, thus far, been delayed by the skill and courage of those dedicated

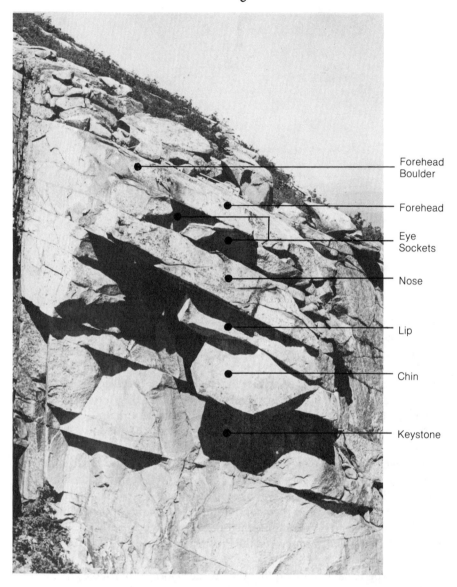

Forehead Boulder

Forehead

Eye Sockets

Nose

Lip

Chin

Keystone

The ledges which form the Old Man viewed from the front.

Saving the Great Stone Face

men who have climbed up to that unprotected height to do repair work on the wondrously arranged rocks!

The Old Man is composed of five ledges, not three as originally thought, and they are placed, with the bottom three which penetrate the mountain, supporting themselves plus the top two which lie on them.

Edward H. Geddes, who did the first repair work in 1916, carefully measured the stones and revised earlier estimates of the size of the granite face. According to Mr. Geddes, and practically identical to recent measurements, the length of the face is 40 feet 5 inches, with a lateral distance of 25 feet in height, the nose 10 feet high, the upper lip 7 feet, and the lower lip and chin together 12 feet high.

Yet figures are forgotten when we look up. As C. H. Hitchcock, state geologist, observed in 1874, the Profile has been "placed by Nature in a very convenient place for exhibition, and in picturesque harmony with its surroundings." In spite of statistics, we admit that our knowledge of the Old Man's origin and formation is rather meager, and we realize that human hands have had no part in his creation.

Franconia Notch Before 1805

FRANCONIA NOTCH was known to white explorers and hunters as early as 1755. Lying in the two townships of Lincoln at the south and Franconia at the north, the Notch was traveled by early settlers on foot and horseback, and later by ox team and horse-drawn wagons. One of the earliest settlers was the Old Man's future discoverer, Luke Brooks. He arrived in 1793 and established a home at what became Copper Cannon Lodge in Franconia.

Edging the sky along the east were the southern peaks of the Franconia Range, including from the south Mounts Flume, Liberty, Haystack, Lincoln, and landslide-scarred Lafayette. On the west side of the Notch were the summits of the Pemigewasset Range, which included Mount Pemigewasset at the south; North and South Kinsman; and then Profile and Cannon mountains, whose lower most northwesterly peak was sometimes known as Jackson.

Discovery of the Profile

DISCOVERY of the Profile is thought to have occurred by accident, as so many important discoveries are. What had been waiting there, unknown for centuries, was suddenly revealed. Following that dramatic

Background Highlights

Saving the Great Stone Face

On the left page are three rarely seen views of the Old Man; the south profile (top left), visible only from the air; a view from above (top right) showing tie rods and turnbuckles, and a startling view (bottom) from directly below his chin. Above is the classic view, an often reproduced photo by C. T. Bodwell.

Background Highlights

moment, it became the central attraction of a whole beautiful mountain region — a focal point of interest to thousands of visitors every year from all over the world.

Previous to the discovery, the Notch road had been hardly more than a rough trail through the forest and underbrush, but the route was fast to become an important link between the North Country farms and the growing Merrimack and seacost towns. In 1805 the state hired Enoch Colby to lay out a road from Woodstock (then called Peeling) to the village of Franconia.

Guy Roberts held that Nathaniel Hall of Thornton worked for Colby and that this was the man who looked up from the shore of Profile Lake while hunting partridges for the road crew's breakfast and discovered the Profile.

Roberts's account is challenged by Sarah N. (Brooks) Welch of Franconia. She relates that her great-grandfather, Luke Brooks, Franconia's tax collector at the time, was the man who discovered the Profile. Her account tells how he and Francis Whitcomb, also of Franconia, were making a survey of land extending from the Notch road up the slopes of Profile and Cannon mountains. Descriptions of the lots adjoining the road were needed for selling them at public auction.

The survey crew, including Brooks and Whitcomb, finished their day's work near the present Tramway parking area. It was getting dark, so the men pitched camp at the upper end of Profile Lake. At that time, both lake and mountain slopes were screened from the road by dense forests, but Brooks and Whitcomb found their way to the sparkling clear lake the next morning to get water for breakfast. As they filled their pails and straightened up, Brooks's gaze wandered up the wooded slope of the mountain rising abruptly from the opposite shore.

The morning sun shone brightly on the high cliffs. Suddenly Luke's eyes widened in amazement. There, sharply outlined high in the blue sky, was the rugged, rock-formed profile of a man's face! Speechless with wonder, he stood in silence for a moment. Then he called his companion to look, and together they stared in wonder at what they saw. One of them whispered, "He looks like President Thomas Jefferson!" — Jefferson was president at the time.

Then they hurriedly brought the other members of the road crew to look up, too, and they soon found that it was only within a certain limited area that the features were in perfect focus. The Profile's first name, Jefferson, was later changed to the Great Stone Face when Nathaniel Hawthorne published his story "The Legend of the Great Stone Face."

Saving the Great Stone Face

Early Travel in Franconia Notch

THE ROAD through Franconia Notch has always been important and has always a subject for discussion on how much to develop it and how much money to spend. Even today, we face the problem of road improvement without doing further ecological harm.

Though it was hardly more than a rough trail for many years, it provided the most direct route from the interior settlements to Boston and Portsmouth where farm products could be exchanged for goods that could not be raised or made at home. Of course, it became even more important after the Old Man was discovered in 1805, and travelers from near and far began making the trip to enjoy the remarkable granite Profile and the Notch's spectacular scenery.

For many years the winding, bumpy journey was made either in summer or in the spring and autumn months when there was the least amount of snow. It was 1813 before the state began to improve the road for the increasing traffic of mountain wagons and later of Concord stagecoaches. In August 1826, during the same storm that devastated Crawford Notch and caused the Willey disaster, the road in Franconia Notch was so badly washed out that it could not be made passable until November. It was not until 1928, with the growing demands of automobile travel and winter sports, that the state kept the Notch open for winter travel. Storms and

The Old Lady of the Mountain, sometimes called The Watcher, is directly across from the Old Man on Eagle Cliff.

Background Highlights

winds have always been factors to reckon with in this lovely Notch of many natural attractions, but they have not discouraged visitors since the Old Man's fame first began to spread.

Flora and Fauna

A S POINTED OUT by Tudor Richards, vegetation on the mountains closely parallels that found in some of the arctic areas of Canada. "The area of the Franconia Range above timberline extends for about two miles in a narrow band along the sharp ridge connecting the summits of Mounts Lincoln and Lafayette," the latter nearly a mile above sea level.

Several northern hardwoods formed dense forests consisting of yellow birch, beech, and sugar maple on the lower slopes. Midway were red spruce, hemlock, and balsam fir, and on the higher slopes just below timberline were dwarfed fir balsam, birch, and mountain ash. Wild game included moose, deer, rabbits, beaver, lynx, otter, fox, wildcat, mink, bear, and fish, with trout, pickerel, salmon, and bass in the lakes and streams.

Franconia Notch remains largely unspoiled and does not differ greatly from what it was before 1805. It continues to shelter some of the finest scenery in our eastern United States, and has become designated by the National Park Service as a natural landmark of both national and international significance.

2

THE OLD MAN BECOMES A MECCA

THE FIRST KNOWN printed information about the Old Man resulted from a letter written by Gen. Martin Field of Newfane, Vermont, to Professor Silliman of the *American Journal of Science and Arts.* The letter was written on November 22, 1827, and consisted of a description and sketch of the Profile. The letter and description will be found in the appendices.

One of the most famous of early visitors to the Old Man was Daniel Webster, a native of Franklin, New Hampshire, and an eloquent United States senator at the time of his visit. In 1831 he was a guest at Ethan Allen Crawford's popular hotel at the head of Crawford Notch. While in the area he rode over to Franconia Notch where he stopped to view the Profile. He is credited with saying of the Great Stone Face, "Men hang out their signs indicative of their respective trades. Shoemakers hang out a gigantic shoe, jewelers a monster watch, and dentists a gold tooth; but up in Franconia Mountains God Almighty has hung out a Sign to show that in New England He Makes Men!"

In the autumn of 1832 one of America's greatest literary figures, Nathaniel Hawthorne, visited the White Mountains. Like Webster, he was a guest at Ethan Allen Crawford's hotel, and like him he visited Franconia Notch and was deeply impressed with the granite Profile. In 1840 he started working on a charming story that developed into his well-known allegorical tale, "The Legend of the Great Stone Face." Written at Salem, Massachusetts, in 1848, the manuscript was submitted to John Greenleaf

15

*Rare view of the short-lived Summit
House on Mount Lafayette about
1865 from an early stereograph.*

*Group photo in the Flume taken by
H. S. Fifield in 1876, typical of the
elegant commercial stereographs he
produced for thirty years*

Whittier, who was then editor of the *National Era*. It was accepted and
appeared in the issue of January 24, 1850. (Hawthorne received just $25
for this famous story.)

Mary Baker Eddy, then Mrs. Mary Glover and later the founder of
Christian Science, was another noted visitor to Franconia Notch, in the
late 1840s. When she alighted from her carriage to get a better view of
the Profile, she was so impressed that she wrote a poem which will be
found in the appendices. The first stanza is as follows:

Old Man of the Mountain

*Gigantic sire, unfallen still thy crest!
Primeval dweller where the wild winds rest,
Beyond the ken of mortal e'er to tell
What power sustains thee in thy rock-bound cell.*

A noted nature-loving clergyman, the Reverend Thomas Starr King,

Saving the Great Stone Face

'inter view in the Flume showing
*e formation was taken for com-
*ercial stereoption sale
*out 1880.

*Looking down into the Flume in
more seasonable temperatures,
circa 1895.*

said this about the Profile: "After a ... shower, ... mists that rise from
the forest below congregate around it ... as if a mighty angel were sit-
ting among the hills and enrobing himself in a cloud vesture."

Another writer, Samuel Adams Drake, wrote of the Profile: "It is the
most extraordinary sight of a lifetime.... It is not merely a face, it is a
portrait.... This gigantic silhouette [is] the greatest curiosity of this or
any other mountain region. — It is unique. This chance jumbling together
of a few stones has produced a sculpture before which Art hangs her head."

Moody Currier, noted as New Hampshire's only poet governor (1884),
also wrote a poem about the Old Man which is included in the appendices.

A variety of visitors have continued to come from all parts of the world
since people beyond the Notch learned about the Old Man. Poets and
other authors, the wise and the humble, have tried to eulogize him; artists have painted his likeness; cameras have clicked; faces have lighted
with wonder and hearts have been stirred with awe at this face. Each viewing is a new and stirring "discovery."

The Old Man Becomes a Mecca

An atmospheric view of the Basin from a glass plate negative made about 1895.

My Own "Discovery"

THE OLD MAN OF THE MOUNTAIN has been an inspiration to me since my high school days in Littleton. It may seem strange, but because my first "discovery" of him must have become an immediate and inseparable part of me, I cannot remember that first time! I know only that with each experience of looking up at him, from a car or from the lake shore, I am deeply stirred and I "discover" him anew!

Since I was of both a musical and a poetic turn of mind, it was inevitable that I should write a song about the Old Man. I was just out of Plymouth Normal School and was in my first year of teaching when the words and music came. I cannot recall which came first; maybe it was the words, or perhaps they came together with the music. I still treasure, in one of my Old Man scrapbooks, the original penciled manuscript of the chorus music dated July 9, 1921, and the scribbled words finished on August 25, 1921.

I had the song copyrighted and published it that same year. It soon became popular and is the first and only "official" song about the Old Man. Two years later, it was sung by a group of my school pupils at the dedication of Franconia Notch as a state memorial park. In 1954 I had a second edition printed and the copyright renewed. It was sung that summer in concerts given by the noted Bretton Woods Boy Singers, founded and directed by Frank R. Hancock (my future husband). In 1955 it was sung again by the Boy Singers at the Old Man's 150th "birthday" celebration attended by President Dwight Eisenhower, state and national dignitaries, and thousands of spectators.

Where We Stand Governs What We See

FOR EACH OF US, whether a longtime admirer or a newcomer looking up at the Old Man for the first time, every new "discovery" reveals not only a noble profile in stone but also an example of the truth that where we choose to stand in life governs what we see. Only within a very limited area is the Profile clearly visible.

According to Leon Anderson, it was the Reverend Benjamin G. Willey of Maine, in his *Incidents in White Mountain History*, published in 1856, who first emphasized that "the Old Man can be seen only from a certain angle." Some years earlier, in 1826, a sign beside the narrow Notch road pointed to the Profile, for it had already been discovered that the face vanishes from view when the observer moves a few yards either left or right of the vantage point. As geologist Hitchcock warned, "It can be seen to advantage only in one line. If you go a short distance either side, the face is distorted and disappears."

With that thought in mind, I close this chapter with a poem of mine written in 1946.

Great Stone Face

Within a small, tree-shadowed space
I can look up and see a Face,
Ice-chiseled long ago.
If I desert that favored sphere,
The noble features disappear
And only ledges show.

It all depends on where I stand
If shapeless rock or something grand
Is visible to me.

The Old Man Becomes a Mecca

*Unusual early view of Professor
John Merrill, "the Old Philosopher,"
in the Pool about 1860.*

*The Sentinel Pine Bridge at the Poo
in the Flume*

*And what I choose to keep in view,
Becomes a part of all I do
And all I hope to be.*

*I'll have to choose with equal care
The stand I take in Life, for there
Within my little place
I'll either see just rock and sky
And never know or wonder why,
Or I'll behold a Face!*

Saving the Great Stone Face

3

THE GOLDEN ERA

A S WITH ANYTHING we own that is of special value, it is not enough to possess and admire it. We should also protect and care for it.

Many early visitors to Franconia Notch began to feel this way about the Profile. As they became more aware of the delicate construction and balance, as well as the grandeur, of this great natural wonder, they realized that the same forces of nature that had created the Old Man could also destroy him. Man, unknowingly, could aid in that destruction.

Growing awareness led interested groups and individuals to promote inspections of the profile-forming rocks. What they found caused a deepening concern, which gradually developed into a threefold purpose: to preserve the Old Man himself, to protect the valley's forests, and to strive for the wise development of the Notch road and public services. These three factors would present problems for many years to come, involving dramatic changes and rival interests.

It is interesting to remember that much of the Notch, including the Old Man, remained in private ownership until 1928. Fortunately two men — Richard Taft and Charles Greenleaf — who owned the largest portion of the valley and mountain slopes, were high-caliber, nature-loving individuals, devoted not only to developing the Notch but also to caring for it.

21

Richard Taft

RICHARD TAFT was born in Barre, Vermont, on March 14, 1812. He grew up on his parents' farm and at the age of eighteen turned to hotel life. He worked in hotels at Nashua, New Hampshire, and Lowell, Massachusetts, and later became landlord of the Washington House in Lowell. During those early years of his busy hotel career, he visited Franconia Notch and was greatly impressed with the possibility of building high-quality hotels in that scenic area. His dreams came true, for he became the successful proprietor of the Lafayette House, the Flume House, and the Profile House, which had been built in 1835, 1848, and 1852, respectively.

Taft died on February 14, 1881, in Littleton, the nearby business center of the White Mountains. He was sixty-nine years old and had won acclaim as one of the Old Man's most devoted disciples.

Five years earlier, in 1876, he had put the Old Man on world display at the centennial of the signing of the Declaration of Independence in Philadelphia. In observance of the occasion an international exposition was held in that city. New Hampshire had the honor of being the ninth state to ratify the nation's Constitution, and Taft wanted something special to represent the Granite State at the exposition. The artist, David Johnson, painted a large, handsome portrait of the Great Stone Face, with Profile Lake at the mountain's base, and Taft arranged for the impressive picture to be framed and given a central spot at the New Hampshire exhibit. In 1890 Mrs. Taft presented the painting to the state library in Concord where it was put on display. It now hangs in the Visitors' Center of the State House.

Charles Greenleaf

COL. CHARLES HENRY GREENLEAF was born July 23, 1841, at Danville, Vermont. Like Taft, he had a strong love for mountain country and was interested in the hotel business at an early age. During his busy career he was connected with prominent hotels in Washington and New York City, and with the Vendome in Boston where he was its proprietor for fifty-five years.

In 1857, when only sixteen, he started work as a bellboy at the new and already famous summer hotel, the Profile House in Franconia Notch. He returned a second season, then worked for a few summers at the noted Crawford House at the head of Crawford Notch, and later returned to

Saving the Great Stone Face

regular summer work at the Profile House.

In the winter of 1865 while he was clerk at the American House in Boston, Richard Taft of the Profile House offered him an interest in his hotel business. Greenleaf accepted, for although he was only twenty-four at the time, he was already devoted to Taft and Franconia Notch and welcomed the opportunity to move to the region. He became a member of the hotel company of Taft, Tyler, and Greenleaf. Four years later, in 1869, Tyler dropped out of the company, and Taft and Greenleaf became partners. When Taft died in 1881, Greenleaf became sole owner-manager of the Profile House. He retired from the hotel business in 1922 when he sold his Franconia Notch hotel property to Frank P. Abbott and Son of nearby Bethlehem. However, tragedy for the Profile House was imminent; in the summer of 1923 it burned to the ground and was never restored.

During those years Greenleaf had established a home in Franconia Village and had taken an active part in local and state affairs. For eleven years he served as treasurer and manager of the Profile & Franconia Notch Railroad; in addition, he was New Hampshire delegate to the 1888 Republican national convention and was an active member of the New England Hotel Association. While a member of the staff of Governor Benjamin F. Prescott, he was given the rank of colonel.

Greenleaf died at the age of eighty-three on May 2, 1924, at Pinehurst, New Jersey. In his will he left $10,000 to the Appalachian Mountain Club;

The first Flume House, circa 1860.

The Golden Era

The second Flume House, circa 1890.

$5,000 to the Dartmouth Outing Club; and $10,000 to the Society for the Protection of New Hampshire Forests, which had been founded in 1901. Probably Greenleaf is best remembered for the Abbie Greenleaf Library which he built in 1912. It was named in honor of his first wife and was donated to the town of Franconia.

His friend, Frank Abbott, who had bought his Notch property, named the thousands of Notch acres Greenleaf Park in his honor, remembering that it was a region he knew and loved so much. Someone else said of this man who so deeply loved nature, "To him she spoke a visible language."

In 1923, the year before he died, Greenleaf prepared a charming little book entitled *History of the Old Man of the Mountain, The Flume — 1857-1920.* I will quote from it in subsequent chapters.

Hotels in Franconia Notch

THROUGH THE EFFORTS of these two men the hotels in Franconia Notch became famous summer vacation centers. These resorts included two hotels at each end of the Notch — the Lafayette and Profile houses at the northern end, the Knight's Tavern and Flume House at the southern.

Saving the Great Stone Face

The original Profile House in the final stages of construction.

The first hotel in Franconia Notch was the Lafayette House. It was built at the site of the present Tramway Valley Station and was named for the nearby mountain. It was opened in 1835 by J. L. Gibbs of Littleton.

At the south end of the Notch another hotel, the Knight's Tavern, was opened for business in 1846. It stood on the west side of the road, nearly opposite the present Flume gateway.

In 1848 the Flume House was built about 1,000 feet north of the former tavern and accommodated guests who came to visit the Flume,* a natural wonder very different from the Old Man at the upper end of the Notch. In 1849 Richard Taft bought the Flume House and the Lafayette House. One year later, when the railroad was extended north from Concord to Plymouth, a stagecoach line began meeting the trains at Plymouth and transporting guests north to the two Notch hotels and beyond. At first, the hotel rate was $1.50 a day; sometime later it was raised to $3.00 a day!

The Flume House was destroyed by fire in 1870, rebuilt in 1872, burned again in 1918, and was never restored.

*The Flume is an unusual rocky chasm 700 feet long and from 10 to 20 feet wide. Flume Brook flows down through the gorge beneath a walkway which provides a safe and delightful opportunity to view this awesome rock formation. The Flume was discovered in 1809 by ninety-three-year-old "Aunt Jess" Guernsey, who was fishing the small stream. Ed.

The Golden Era

Remodeled Profile House and cottages in the 1890s.

The Lafayette House at the north of the Notch was the predecessor of the famous Profile House which was built in 1852. It was a popular resort for seventy-one years until August 9, 1923, when it, too, became a smoldering heap of charred wood and twisted metal.

The Profile House

O F ALL THE NOTCH HOTELS, the Profile House was the most intimately related to the great Profile for which it was named. Both its years of elegance and popularity and its final destruction were important in the Old Man's destiny.

The first Profile House was built by Richard Taft after he took over the large acreage of Notch property from the Gibbs Company. He converted the Lafayette House into a dormitory for employees and constructed a four-story hotel with 110 rooms. In 1866 a large addition twice the size of that building was constructed, and two years later the first of twenty-nine cottages was built along a terrace at the rear. Taft also constructed large red stables for 350 horses used for the fleet of carriages, coaches, mountain wagons, and horseback riding, and erected a blacksmith shop for shoeing the horses.

Four years later, in 1872, with Taft and Greenleaf as proprietors, there

Saving the Great Stone Face

were more additions and improvements, including a large dining room. Other attractions were gas lamps, post and telegraph offices, gift and barber shops, a 100 by 50 foot parlor, private baths, billiard halls and bowling alleys, and an orchestra. For outdoor recreation there were such activities as fishing, swimming, boating, trail hiking, burro riding, and golfing on the hotel's private course.

Taft died in 1881, leaving Greenleaf the sole owner. Since the hotel, once more, could not accommodate the growing business, Greenleaf decided to tear it down during the autumn of 1905. Under his personal supervision a crew of 300 worked through the winter and spring, with the result that the new and larger Profile House was ready by July 1, 1906. It was a luxuriously appointed four-story frame building with 400 rooms. The main lobby was about 250 feet long; the walls and carpeting were a Pompeian red; and large plate-glass windows looked out on both sides. The main dining room, octagonal in shape, could seat 600 people; it had a domed ceiling 35 feet high with no supporting columns. There was a water-powered elevator, and sparkling spring water was piped from a mountain brook which tumbled down from its source high on the mountainside.

The menus were attractive four-page folders with pictures and descriptions of local points of interest on the front and back covers, and lists

The Golden Era

Made in England by an unidentified manufacturer, this is presumably a special edition pitcher and a fine example of the souvenir and hotel china of the period.

of wines and dinner suggestions on the inside. A typical menu included: Wines: 15 choices of champagne, 9 claret, 13 Rhine and Moselle, 4 white wines, 6 Burgundy, 12 Madeira, 8 sherry, 5 port, 7 American wines, 12 brandies, 5 ales—also liqueurs, cordials, and mineral waters. Dinner offered soups, fish, 3 boiled or 5 roasted meats, 3 cold meats, 6 hot meats, 12 vegetables, 12 relishes, five puddings and pastries, 12 desserts, and tea and coffee.

A small, delightfully informative folder, *Profile Events*, was printed daily. In it were sports announcements, programs of concerts by the Boston Symphony Orchestra musicians who played twice daily through the week and every Sunday evening, lists of guests in residence, a section "What the Old Man Sees," and other items of interest, all for 75 cents for six weeks or 15 cents for a single copy.

Of particular interest was a cannon near Echo Lake which was used for special sound effects. There was a fee of 50 cents per blast for any guest wishing to enjoy the reverberating thunder as it echoed and reechoed among the mountains.

The handsome, well-appointed hotel complex was "one of the most famous of summer resort hotels in America. The fine appointments, cuisine, opportunities for amusements of various kinds, social life, and other features have always attracted refined and cultured people."

Saving the Great Stone Face

Even the young people enjoyed coming back, year after year, and many of them "grew up" in the summers which they enjoyed with their parents and other guests. Lifelong friendships were made, and treasured experiences were shared through the years. One childhood prank was recorded by J. Holland Beal. There was a beautiful bed of red geraniums in the middle of the turnaround in front of Profile Hotel. On one occasion, when shoes were placed outside room doors at night for cleaning and polishing as usual, in the morning each one was found with a red geranium blossom in it!

Lasting impressions were made on young minds when the children looked up at the Great Stone Face. Nathaniel Hawthorne expressed it well when he wrote: "It was a happy lot for children to grow up to manhood and womanhood with the Great Stone Face before their eyes, for all the features were noble, and the expression was at once grand and sweet, as if it were the glow of a vast, warm heart that embraced all mankind in its affections. It was an education only to look at it."

One guest described his stirring experience of walking out alone from the Profile House in the hush of an early morning. It was William Cooper Prime, noted editor, author, art expert, and world traveler who said, "Six hundred persons were sleeping in the Profile House ... but ... Franconia Notch might have been as desolate as it was two hundred years ago.... If you never saw mountains wake out of the darkness ... you have something to see in the world yet."

Leaving the Profile House for the Flume in the 1870s.

The Golden Era

Original dining room of the first Profile House, noteworthy for the elegance of its decor and appointments.

Arrival of President U. S. Grant

OF ALL THE ARRIVALS of famous guests at the Profile House, probably that of President Ulysses S. Grant was the most spectacular and exciting. He made his dramatic appearance late in the day on August 27, 1869. (This was the same year the famous Cog Railway was completed to the top of Mount Washington, about twenty-five miles from Franconia Notch and a point of interest to the president before his historic ride to the Profile House.) Ernest A. Barney's account of the president's visit is included here, in part.

In August, 1869, General Grant, having begun his first administration as President, and finding himself in need of a vacation, determined to make a flying trip through the principal points of interest in the White Mountains. The weather elsewhere was hot, the mountains were cool, and he had never visited them.

Saving the Great Stone Face

The Profile House raised its own grapes here, and had its own trout pond, dairy and farm.

The President accordingly started with a party of about 25 and made a brief tour of the mountains, reaching Bethlehem, 11 miles from the Profile House, on the 27th. He stopped at the Sinclair House, from which point he was to be conveyed to the Profile House by carriage.

When General Grant reached Bethlehem, word was telegraphed to the Profile House that he was waiting to be taken over. At that time a man by the name of Edmund Cox carried people from the hotel to the Flume, one of the sights of the mountains. For this purpose he drove a large coach, resembling a bandwagon, capable of seating 16 people. [It was the posh Flume Stagecoach, painted yellow with supple springs and a high box seat in front.] Mr. Cox sat up there and held the reins. [He was the most skillful and daring driver in the mountains.]

Cox liked the best of horses and always owned them. These eight beauties stood in their places in front of the Flume Coach as the last finishing touches were being given preparatory to the start [to meet the President in Bethlehem].

The Golden Era

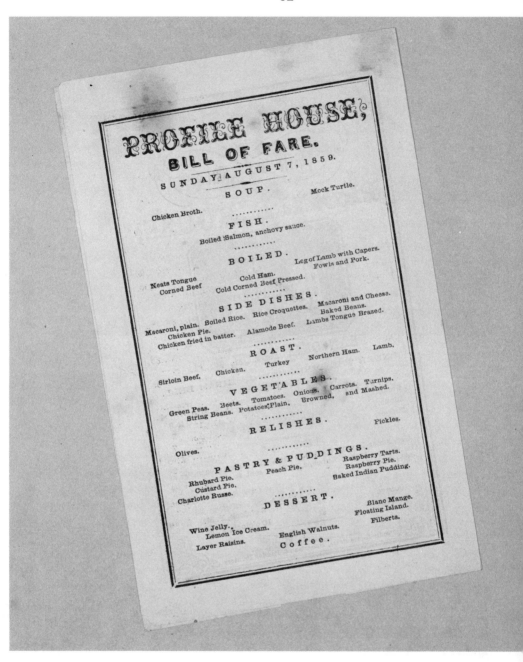

PROFILE HOUSE,
BILL OF FARE.
SUNDAY, AUGUST 7, 1859.

SOUP.

Chicken Broth.   Mock Turtle.

FISH.

Boiled Salmon, anchovy sauce.

BOILED.

Leg of Lamb with Capers.
Fowls and Pork.

Neats Tongue   Cold Ham.
Corned Beef   Cold Corned Beef Pressed.

SIDE DISHES.

Macaroni, plain. Boiled Rice. Rice Croquettes.   Macaroni and Cheese.
          Chicken Pie.   Baked Beans.
Chicken fried in batter.   Alamode Beef.   Lambs Tongue Brazed.

ROAST.

                         Turkey   Northern Ham.   Lamb.
Sirloin Beef.   Chicken.

VEGETABLES.

Green Peas.   Beets.   Tomatoes.   Onions.   Carrots.   Turnips.
     String Beans.   Potatoes Plain,   Browned,   and Mashed.

RELISHES.

                                                    Pickles.

Olives.

PASTRY & PUDDINGS.

                         Peach Pie,   Raspberry Tarts.
     Rhubard Pie.   Raspberry Pie.
       Custard Pie.   Baked Indian Pudding.
Charlotte Russe.

DESSERT.

                                              Blanc Mange.
                                           Floating Island.
Wine Jelly.   Filberts.
   Lemon Ice Cream.   English Walnuts.
Layer Raisins.   Coffee.

Saving the Great Stone Face

About 3 o'clock Cox started, and jogged along easily toward Bethlehem. It was one of the important occasions of his life, and he felt it. But he did not propose to wear out his horses by useless haste, until the time came. It was 11 miles to Bethlehem [over steep and bumpy roads] but by judicious management this would be only the better for the animals, and fit them for the grand effort to come.

When, about 7 o'clock of that calm August evening, the Presidential party stepped out of the Sinclair House, General Grant's trained eye swept over the team with the glance of a connoisseur and at once recognized its excellence.

Walking quickly to the driver's seat, he said to Cox, "If you have no objection, I will get up there with you." "It is pretty rough riding up here," was the reply. "I can stand it if you can," said Grant as he climbed up beside Cox and settled himself.

The President was dressed in a high silk hat, black suit, and a long linen duster that covered as much of his clothing as possible. The others in the party climbed inside and all was ready.

The driver tightened the reins with a "Whist!" and with a spring in perfect unison, the animals were off for the Profile House. The telegraph operator at the Sinclair sat with finger on the key, looking out the window and watching for the moment of the start. A message at once flashed over the wire to the Profile House, and the time was noted. It was precisely 7 o'clock.

At the Profile [House] a large company had gathered in the office and on the porch, awaiting the arrival. Among them were several stage drivers who knew every foot of the road and said Cox could not make it in less than two hours, or two and a half hours. The last three miles [Three Mile Hill] were right up into the Notch, with a steep grade all the way. But Cox, as they knew, intended to break all records if he could.

Echo Lake is about a quarter of a mile from the Profile House. A cannon was waiting, with a man ready to fire it off as the Presidential coach swept past. There would be three blasts to let the people at the Profile House know he was coming.

At the hotel, all were listening for the signal. Suddenly, Bang! went the cannon! No one could believe it was the President. "Look at the time! It can't be! Some mistake has been made!" Then the cannon banged twice more. It was the Presidential party!

In what seemed to be an incredibly short time, they heard the tramping of the flying steeds and the rattle of the coach, and in another moment they swept around the corner of the hotel into view.

The Golden Era

The second Profile House which took the place of its predecessor, torn down in 1900. Landslide scars on Mount Lafayette are clearly visible to the left.

Ed Cox stood up on the footboard, with teeth set, eyes blazing, and every rein drawn tight in his hands. General Grant sat beside him, holding his hat with one hand, and the other grasping the seat. The eight horses were on the full run, with mouths wide open, ears back flat to their heads, and nostrils distended. They were covered with sweat and foam, yet all under control of the magician on the box. As they made the circle and drew up in front of the hotel, Cox threw his weight on the brakes and stopped at once. He had made the trip in precisely 58 minutes!

General Grant, as he dismounted from his lofty perch, was a curious spectacle. Covered with dust from head to foot, he had the appearance of a man who had been rolled in the road. Hat, hair, and whiskers had suffered alike, and including his clothing he was all dust color.

A spectator later said, "S'pose you've heard tell that them hosses run every inch of the road. Well, they didn't, not by my galluses they didn't. They just floo, actooly floo over the road. Half the time the wheels of the stage were just spinnin' in the air when they rounded the curves!"

General Grant [was so impressed that he] sent Cox a Christmas gift

Saving the Great Stone Face

the following December in recognition of his admiration of skill exhibited on that record-breaking ride. The gift was an ornate whip. The ebony stock was four feet in length, showing many silver ferrules, with a last of finely braided pig-skin 12 feet long, and the whole thing enclosed in a velvet-lined morocco case. The center of the covering was ornamented by a silver plate with the name "Edmund K. Cox, Franconia, N.H."

The next day the president proceeded by carriage at a "more leisurely pace" to see the Old Man, who, according to reports, "was as serene as though ready for that special occasion."

But not all was serene with the Old Man. Invisible forces of nature were at work, in spite of the apparent durability of the majestic rock formation. Many more people, the great and the humble, would come to gaze upward, and many years would go by, before the real seriousness of the problem was discovered and something done about it.

In the meantime, travel to the Profile House was aided by the huffing and puffing of steam trains right into Franconia Notch!

Trains in Franconia Notch

IN THE SUMMER of 1878 the Profile & Franconia Notch Railroad Company was granted a charter by the New Hampshire legislature to build a narrow-gauge steam car line from Sawyer's (now Pierce's) Bridge at Bethlehem Junction to the Profile House in Franconia Notch, a distance of nine miles. Two steam engines, the *Profile* and the *Echo*, pulled a usual load of one baggage and one passenger car. These trains connected at the junction with overnight limiteds from New York City, Boston, and Portland which arrived on the Wing Road branch of the Boston, Concord & Montreal Railroad.

In 1891 the Profile & Franconia Notch Railroad was taken over by the Boston, Concord & Montreal Railroad, which continued until 1897 when the mountain run was converted into standard gauge with steel rails. During the mid 1890s, the Boston, Concord & Montreal line was bought by the Boston & Maine Railroad, which operated until the run was abandoned.

The last train to Profile House made the trip in the fall of 1920. The following year, because the rails were getting so rusted in the Notch, the Boston & Maine asked permission to abandon the line. Abandonment was granted, and the handsome little station near the Profile House later became the Notch Gift Shop of the New Hampshire League of Arts and Crafts.

The Golden Era

The narrow-guage Profile & Franconia Notch Railroad depot at the Profile House.

Saving the Great Stone Face

The locomotive "Profile" and coach with its train crew after the railroad was converted to standard guage in the 1890s.

An era had passed; automobiles were taking the place of trains.

Part of the route is still visible from a point on Trudeau Road, and a section of U.S. Route 3 was constructed on part of the former right-of-way. Even today one can almost hear those sturdy little steam engines chugging along and whistling their warning at the crossings. At the former terminal site one can imagine the lively scenes of arriving and departing guests, with their many trunks and other baggage, back in those nostalgic days when the Profile House was in its heyday, a romantic era indeed, and still remembered by a lucky few.

The Golden Era

The Flume
Samuel L. Gerry, before 1883
37" x 21"
Oil on canvas
Collection: New Hampshire Historical Society

II

The
Troubled
Years

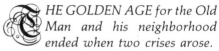

HE GOLDEN AGE for the Old Man and his neighborhood ended when two crises arose.

No one had ever dreamed that the Old Man's well-being might be threatened until sometime around the Civil War when a young man who was staying at the Profile House made frequent trips up to the Profile. He soon discovered that natural forces — freezing temperatures, snow, rain, and ice — had moved the large stone constituting the foremost part of the forehead ahead from its parent rock. It was evident that this movement had to be halted, and since that time dedicated men have striven to preserve the Old Man.

Equally dangerous to the Profile and the neighboring Notch was the unexpected "Outrage of 1893" when lumbermen suddenly erected unsightly sawmills and shanties below the Basin and started cutting wide swaths through the forest. The unsightly destruction marked the beginning of a never-ending battle to preserve the Notch from private interests.

This occurred at a time when the nation was wasting its natural resources, fouling its rivers, destroying its prairies and forests, and expanding its smoky and congested cities. Many had no thought of the future, for the Industrial Revolution was triumphing over the old agrarian way of life, and much of industry was riding roughshod over the natural resources of the nation.

Many people in New Hampshire, however, were alert to the dangers. Fully aware of the beauty, importance, and value of their precious natural resources in the White Mountains, they were determined to preserve what they had from fundamentally destructive development. Eight years after the "Outrage of 1893" the Society for the Protection of New Hampshire Forests was established, and ten years later it was a New Hampshire senator who was instrumental in persuading Congress to enact the precedent-setting Weeks Act.

Unfortunately, all this was to prove only a holding action, one of many efforts to save Franconia Notch and its Profile, which seemed destined to be the frequent target of unfriendly forces.

4

WARNINGS OF THE 1870s

A T THIS TIME, amid the happy bustle and the elaborate attention paid to hotel guests, certain longtime friends of the Great Stone Face were becoming aware that all was not well with him. Col. Charles Greenleaf, proprietor of the Profile House, was one of the first to heed the warnings. His little book, published in 1923 and mentioned earlier, voices his concern.

For many years, having been asked by interested friends regarding my knowledge and observations of the "Old Man of the Mountain," I now deem it best to record some facts and recollections which cluster around the "Great Stone Face," which for over sixty years has been of great interest to me during my stay in Franconia Notch.

Further along he writes:

Although the time of its creation is unknown, yet the Lord placed it where a Christian people might be strengthened in their faith at beholding one of His mighty works. Had it been placed in an unenlightened land, it might have become an idol ... and been a "stone of stumbling" to many people.

As a young man I began my long stay at the Profile House in 1857. Boy-like, of course, I made many excursions to all the points of interest, including a trip to the head of the "Old Man," in which I became very

41

The Profile House boathouse on
Profile Lake.

Solitude on Profile Lake in th
1870s . .

much interested, studying carefully the formation and position of the wide-
ly separated rocks which from a distance of twelve hundred feet below,
at Profile Lake, form the profile of a human face. Since then I have made
many visits there, but from the first I noticed that the large stone which
forms the foremost part of the forehead, had at some time, or in some
way, moved forward from the parent rock, the contour of the edges show-
ing that they had formerly been joined together.

After the passing of many years, I read in a Boston paper the state-
ment that those who wished to see the "Old Man of the Mountain" had
better hasten their visit there, as the face was in evident danger of falling
into the valley below.

Mr. Greenleaf does not give the date of the newspaper article, but it
probably was one of the several accounts that appeared in the 1870s when
members of the Appalachian Mountain Club made their examinations,
the first time in 1872.

Greenleaf continues:

At that time I was one of the partners and the Manager of the firm

Saving the Great Stone Face

. and in the 1890s

The Profile Spring house
before 1900.

of Taft and Greenleaf, owners of the Profile and Flume Hotels properties, and, of course, was very much disturbed at reading such an article. A short time after this I engaged one of the best stone masons to be found in the north country, and accompanied by a blacksmith and two or three other men, left the hotel in the early morning for a trip to the "Old Man's" head with the idea of determining if there were any such danger, and if so, if there were anything that could be done to prevent such a national calamity.

The immensity in size and weight of the rocks convinced us that it was useless to try to preserve the "Old Man of the Mountain" as a whole, and personally I have always believed that the whole formation would some day all go together, as farther back of the head are seams in the rock, which would indicate that the trouble would begin there, and precluded the possibility of doing anything to preserve the face intact. But regarding the so-called forehead stone, notwithstanding the many suggestions received, I waited for a better solution or remedy before doing anything.

In 1872 the Appalachian Mountain Club reported that according to its examination it had pinpointed the Old Man's location and discovered

Warnings of the 1870s

the precarious position of the forehead boulder which had moved away from the forehead proper and was hanging in space. The report aroused many other people besides Greenleaf. One man, the Reverend Guy Roberts of Whitefield, later wrote a little book, *The Profile and How It Was Saved*, in which he said:

Certain members of the Appalachian Mountain Club located the profile-forming ledges accurately, and in doing so discovered that one of the large stones which form the prominent part of the forehead was in danger of falling off. The discovery was written up and printed in several publications at the time, and a further examination was made by the proprietor of the Profile House, accompanied by a stone mason and a blacksmith, with the decision that owing to the size of the rock nothing could be done to "save the Old Man." . . . Here the matter was dropped and in the main forgotten.

As Niels Nielsen wrote just 100 years later, "Though people fretted over this situation, it was not until 1906 that Reverend Guy Roberts of Whitefield climbed to the Old Man and observed the danger to the Profile itself should the forehead stone fall and strike the nose."

Roberts studied the rock formation with a powerful glass; then, on September 5, 1906, he climbed to the brow for a detailed examination. His firsthand survey, which included photographs, revived concern for the Old Man's longevity, for he confirmed what the AMC members had found thirty-four years earlier.

Guy Roberts was not one to give up easily. Although the owners of the mountain, the Profile and Flume Hotels Company, believed nothing could be done, Roberts stumped the state for ten years to raise support for the Old Man's preservation.

Earlier, in the 1890s, another kind of danger had appeared in Franconia Notch. The beautiful forest lands were being denuded. The danger was not only to the lovely natural setting of the Old Man; it was also to the several mountain streams that had their sources high on the wooded slopes and were sheltered for many miles as the important headwaters of the Pemigewasset and Merrimack river valleys.

Saving the Great Stone Face

5

OUTRAGE, 1893

M Y INFORMATION regarding this menace was found at the Bethlehem Library in some rare old copies of the *White Mountain Echo,* a weekly newspaper of the 1890s.

An editorial entitled "Vandalism" appeared July 1, 1893. It related that "ruthless lumbermen have invaded Franconia Notch." Their presence was marked not only by the felling of trees in wide swaths but also by the unsightly sawmills and several shanties (living quarters for the lumbermen) on both sides of the road. This "foul blotch on the fair face of Nature" was found in 1893 between the Profile and Flume houses a few rods below the Basin, a natural pool in the swift Pemigewasset.

The devastation was

due to the action of Mr. M. F. Whitehouse of Concord, who purchased timber on a large tract extending from the banks of the Pemigewasset to the summits of the mountain range. Proprietors of the adjoining proper-ty were ready to purchase the portion near the brook and road but couldn't due to the present owner's determination to take timber from the west side of Franconia Range and saw it at mills erected near the stream, which will then be doubly damaged by casting sawdust into it.

The writer of the editorial hoped that this devastation would alert New Hampshire to the danger that would result "if some united effort is not made to stay the hand of the destroyer of natural attractions." The editor

Looking north through the Notch from Mount Lafayette, circa 1918.

concluded, "The New Hampshire Legislature in its last session moved to preserve the White Mountain forests, but there should also be a statute to regulate cutting of timber and prevent unsightly buildings and pollution of streams."

The following week, another long article in the *Echo* appeared under the "Franconia Notch Outrage." It concluded with comments from the *Concord Monitor* and the *Boston Herald.* Evidently there had been some swift action in stopping the "vandalism." It was announced that

the owner [probably Colonel Greenleaf] of all the property along the Notch road, with the exception of the tract already ravaged by lumbermen, had purchased 50 acres of devastated property lying by the roadside and will, so far as possible, remove the blotch now so offensive. It is hoped the unsightly sawmill and lumbermen's shanties will be demolished without delay, but it will be years before tree stumps will be hidden by new growth. Purchasing land after it is denuded is like locking the barn after the horse is stolen!

The price paid for the fifty acres along the roadside was $5,000. Removal of the trees was "a loss to the State and an offense to the eyes,"

Saving the Great Stone Face

as well as a menace to travelers, because hauling timber to the railroad station at North Woodstock was so destructive to the road that it made it dangerous. One man reported that he was all but thrown from his buggy a little south of the Flume House. The horse and vehicle sank "about three feet into the mud for about 12 feet, then for a distance of four miles struggled through more mud and holes. It will be a big expense to the State to keep that section of road in repair."

The *Concord Monitor* complimented the editor of the *Echo* who, it stated, "has blown a trumpet blast that will reverberate far and wide and encourage crusaders to work against wholesale destruction of forests in New Hampshire." It said the defacement "had come at an opportune time — a deed necessary to arouse public attention to the needs of forestry legislation."

The *Boston Herald* called the Notch road between the Profile House and the Flume House "the loveliest carriage road in the White Mountains. Lumbermen have gone into Franconia Notch and blotched this delightful driveway by cutting the forest clear, a few rods below the Basin, and carried devastation far up the mountain to eastward."

The *Echo* announced that comments on "vandalism" were to be expected at a field meeting of the Appalachian Mountain Club at Jefferson when the state forest commission and leading Appalachians were to hold a joint conference, "but much damage has already been done."

It had been the boast of Colonel Greenleaf that the Notch area was safe, and thousands of dollars had been spent on making the ride through it attractive. Convinced that they were protected, no mountain landlords had appeared before the New Hampshire legislature the previous winter to plead for preservation of forests and for a statute to regulate timber cutting.

The *Herald* article concluded, "At present there is no power in New Hampshire to prevent such devastation except use of right of public domain, which the present forestry law allows the Commission to invoke at the request of persons wishing the protection of certain spots. The wise and beneficial treatment of New Hampshire forests has hardly begun!"

Evidently the "Outrage of 1893" did stir up public determination to do something. In 1901 the Society for the Protection of New Hampshire Forests was founded, and on March 1, 1911, the National Forest Act, promoted by Senator Weeks of New Hampshire, became law.

However, the exciting year of 1893 would not be the last time that Franconia Notch had to be saved from the lumberman's ax. Another and even broader threat was yet to come.

Outrage, 1893

The viewing place and the Old Man, circa 1918.

Saving the Great Stone Face

The Reverend Guy Roberts to the Profile's Rescue

NOT ONLY had there been an alert to the need for the preservation of the forests in the Notch, but by 1906 Rev. Guy Roberts had started a persistent campaign to preserve the Old Man.

Nearly ten years went by before he finally got results. "And still," as he wrote in his book, "the Profile awaits its hastening doom." His trip to the top of the Profile in 1906, and his report to the proprietors of the Profile House, went unheeded because it was believed nothing could be done.

But Roberts could not accept that idea. It did not seem possible that "the bigness of the slipping rock and its inaccessibility were sufficient reasons for standing by and allowing what had been styled 'the American Wonder of the World to go to pieces.' " He believed that it could be permanently secured by means of lewis blocks and the like. However, not being a stoneman, and knowing his opinion would not carry weight, he hoped to find a competent quarryman and take him up onto the head to make an examination and suggest the proper method of fastening.

Finally he found the right man. In August 1915 E.H. Geddes, manager of the C.H. Hardwick Company's granite quarry in Quincy, Massachusetts, happened to be visiting relatives in Littleton, next to Whitefield. Geddes and Roberts had already met, so it was soon arranged for Geddes to make the examination, with Roberts, and to submit a report of what he thought could be done.

As a result of the examination and report in 1915, action was at last taken by the state to have preservation work done on the Old Man's forehead. The first step had been made in saving the Great Stone Face!

Sketch by artist Claude L. Brusseau of Littleton who, in his career, has almost certainly drawn and painted the Old Man in more ways and more often than any other person. Note the use of the plural "mountains" . . . a subject of considerable debate.

Outrage, 1893

6

FIRST REPAIRS ON THE PROFILE

THREE MEN played important roles in the first repairs on the Great Stone Face. They were Col. Charles Greenleaf, the Reverend Guy Roberts, and quarryman Edward H. Geddes.

Colonel Greenleaf was the first to discover that there had been slippage of the forehead stone. Shortly after 1857 he made the startling discovery during one of his many trips from the Profile House to the top of the face. For a long time he believed that nothing could be done, and that was the general opinion of everyone who knew of the danger.

The Reverend Guy Roberts was the first to be convinced that something *could* be done, and he worked until he found the right man to do it.

Edward Geddes was the determined, courageous man who supplied the workable plan and did the "surgery" that secured the slipping forehead stone to the main ledge. According to his daughter, Mabelle (Geddes) Russell, of Littleton, Edward H. Geddes of Quincy, Massachusetts, was born in New Brunswick on October 25, 1863. As a young man he went to Quincy and became associated with the granite industry.

He was superintendent of two Quincy quarries, C. H. Hardwick and Co. from 1900 to 1929, and the Granite Railway Company from 1929 to 1939 when he retired due to ill health. The Granite Railway Co. quarry is remembered because of its historical importance. Here the first [commercial] railroad in America was built to carry granite from the quarry to the Neponset River. From there the granite was transported by barge to Charlestown to build the Bunker Hill Monument.

Geddes's meeting with Roberts and their first trip to the top of the profile is recorded in Geddes's own handwriting (in a manuscript among the scrapbook papers given by Mabelle to the Littleton Area Historical Society).

In 1915 I was compelled to take a rest on account of ill health. I went to Littleton to my wife's sister and her husband, Mr. and Mrs. E. C. Emery. There I met the Reverend Guy Roberts who asked my opinion about fastening this rock. After some explanation I expressed a desire to see it and we agreed to go up there. I think it was the following day or two days later. We made the journey by rail, as the Profile Railroad [from Bethlehem Junction] was then in operation to the Profile House. Then we went up the mountain. It was a very warm day and I could not go very fast, but after several hours we reached the head and he explained to me the parts that formed the chin, lips, nose and forehead. I had never seen the profile from any angle before. After looking it over my first thought was to put it [the slipping forehead stone] on hinges — I mean, to fasten it so when the ice lifted it up one inch or one foot, it would come back to its original position when the ice thawed out. I explained this to Reverend Roberts who didn't seem to understand, so I told him I would make a model for him. We wended our way back down the mountain and he took me down to Profile Lake. I tell you I have never gazed on anything in my life that has caused the same feeling in me as when I gazed at that Stone Face and I will never forget it. I asked God in His goodness to show me the right way to preserve this wonder, and when I got home I started at once to make the model of the way I thought it should be fastened. I made a model [of wood and brass] showing how the holes should be drilled and how the stone could be safely and effectively fastened. When I made this I did not expect to do the work. I sent it to Roberts, telling him if anyone could produce a better plan to accept it.

His daughter Mabelle goes into further detail about the forehead stone and model in her book mentioned previously.

To see this boulder, which forms the forehead, and the position it occupies on the side of the mountain, is to wonder how it has remained there.

First Repairs on the Profile

The small front or profile-forming end rests on the ledge beneath it but the large back end, not seen from below, is hanging in space well off the ledge. This huge boulder, estimated to weigh 25 tons, is 19 feet long and 5 feet wide. The small end is 3 feet 6 inches deep, the back end is 5 feet 7 inches deep. It shows very plainly by its contour that originally it was back against the parent ledge.

Each winter the snow and ice, freezing, thawing, then freezing again, in the fracture between the boulder and the parent ledge, were slowly but surely pushing the 25 ton boulder off the ledge. Due to its position on the mountain side the boulder was being pushed in two directions at the same time, forward as the mountain slopes downward, and endwise as the large back end is considerably higher than the small profile-forming end. Originally the Old Man must have had a somewhat retreating forehead when the boulder was back against the parent rock, but with the outward movement the forehead has assumed the massive proportion it shows today.

After examining the forehead boulder, Father thought the best method to stop its movement would be to use turnbuckles and half lewises, in other words to put the boulder on hinges. This would be done by fastening one end of the hinge to the moving boulder, the other end to the parent rock. In this way, when the loose boulder was lifted or pushed by the freezing action, it must come back to the original position when the ice melted out.

During the following winter he made a brass and wood model. The turnbuckles, rods, and half lewises were sawed out of a solid piece of brass, then fastened into small blocks of wood representing the boulder and the parent rock. I remember well the evenings Father spent in his cellar workshop. Early in March 1916 he sent the model to Mr. Roberts.

Roberts, in turn, sent a letter to Colonel Greenleaf. Mabelle's book quotes an extract from the letter:

Whitefield, June 17, 1916

The Quincy Quarry Manager to whom I referred has made a complete investigation, together with a little brass and wood model showing just how it could be easily, safely, and effectively done, and has placed all this in my hands. He has a perfectly feasible plan for preventing this stone from ever slipping off — as it certainly will do eventually if left to it-

Saving the Great Stone Face

self. . . . I would like to come to Profile as soon as possible and show you the model and talk the matter over with you.

Greenleaf's book continues the story:

Shortly after this, Mr. Roberts came to Profile House and I examined the model carefully, and, as President of the Profile and Flume Hotels Co., agreed to have the work done if sanctioned by our Directors. As President, I realized that while the "Great Stone Face" was located on our property, it was also of State and National interest as well, and for me to undertake anything that might endanger the loss or cause the disfigurement of the Profile, and possibly the loss of life or limb while the work was being done, should be carefully considered.

A few days later I wrote to Governor Roland H. Spaulding stating my views of what should be done to preserve the "Old Man of the Mountain." At the same time I asked him if it would be convenient to have me send Mr. Roberts to appear before him and his Council with the working model of a plan that had my approval. The Governor appointed a day, and after their meeting the Governor promptly and courteously wrote me expressing his ready willingness to join in the expense and approved such an undertaking, if I would assume entire charge of the work necessary to be done.

Mabelle has this to say of the meeting with the governor:

Mr. Roberts had taken pictures of the forehead boulder, and made a plaster model of the Profile showing the slipping boulder fastened to the parent rock using the brass turnbuckles made by Mr. Geddes. All this data was taken to Concord for the meeting with the Governor and his Council.

Upon receipt of the governor's letter, Greenleaf started work as quickly as possible. As he said in his book,

I feared that it was too late in the Autumn for such an undertaking. My experience at Profile House had shown that the thermometer invariably registers below the freezing point before October 1st, and a light fall of snow is not infrequent.

First Repairs on the Profile

Top: Geddes examining the forehead stone during his first visit in 1915.

Above: Robert's plaster model with Geddes' brass turnbuckles which went before Governor Spaulding and his Council.

Left: A precarious perch on the forehead stone during that same first visit.

Saving the Great Stone Face

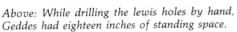

Above: While drilling the lewis holes by hand, Geddes had eighteen inches of standing space.

Top right: Two of the three turnbuckle assemblies in place: total weight of all three, 450 pounds.

Right: During the work tourists at Profile Lake would blow their automobile horns and wave at Geddes until he waved back.

First Repairs on the Profile

Above: A triumphant salute from the face at the completion of the work.

Left: Geddes daughter Mabelle accompanied her father to the top in later years when he checked his work. This pensive photo was taken in September, 1928.

Saving the Great Stone Face

Mabelle continued the story:

By this time it was September, too late in the season for the undertaking of such a task. Mountain weather is very unpredictable, and at this time of year can change rapidly. One day may be warm and sunny while the following day is cold and blustery with a light fall of snow possible. However, it was decided to go ahead with the work due to the worry over the Old Man's impending doom. Measurements taken had shown that the forehead boulder had only some four inches to move before it would be overbalanced. To quote Colonel Greenleaf, "We were most fortunate in securing the services of Mr. Geddes, who was deeply interested and expressed a willingness not only to place the turnbuckles in proper position but to do all the drilling necessary, and which must be perfectly done. A less courageous or unskilled man could not have completed the job."

The three turnbuckles, rods, and half lewises used in fastening the slipping boulder were manufactured by the O. V. Hooker & Co., St. Johnsbury, Vt. They were made of Bessemer steel, weighing altogether about 450 pounds and measuring in length 3 feet 9 inches, 5 feet 6 inches, and 6 feet 3 inches, the variation in length being due to the distances of the forehead boulder from the parent rock. They were to be installed at a 45 degree angle due to the position of the forehead and the supporting ledge underneath the boulder.

Briefly, a turnbuckle is constructed and works as follows. At each extreme end is a half lewis which is inserted into the granite. A half lewis is one inch wider at the bottom than at the top; one side is straight, the other side is slanting. A straight key is then driven in on the straight side of the half lewis so that a dovetail grip results, which is impossible to pull out. Then a rod is connected, by a clevis, through an eye in the top end of the half lewis and an eye in one end of the rod. The other end of the rod is threaded, this being the buckle connecting end. The buckle, which is in the center, is threaded inside on each end, one end being a right thread, the other a left thread. When the buckle is screwed on to the rods there is a tightening action by which all the parts are brought to the exact length required.

Mr. Geddes was 53 years of age when he came to the Profile, the end of September 1916, to do the work. This was publicized in the Boston newspaper and in some New Hampshire ones. The Boston Post also carried the story of how Mr. Geddes had just quarried, from the C. H. Hardwick Co. quarry where he was superintendent, the largest single block

First Repairs on the Profile

of granite ever taken from the quarries in Quincy. It measured 200 feet long, 75 feet wide, and 15 feet thick.

The Profile House was closed for the season but Lafayette Cottage was still open. Here, on September 24, [1916,] he met Colonel Greenleaf for the first time. Later that evening Mr. Roberts arrived. The next morning Mr. Roberts went up the mountain with Mr. Geddes to be sure he knew the way from the top down the 800 feet to the head. It was difficult to locate the forehead boulder unless one knew exactly what to look for. After spending some time taking pictures, Mr. Roberts left Mr. Geddes to his labors, [he] returning the day the work was completed.

The following account is quoted by Mabelle as taken directly from the manuscript of her brave and determined father. He had a heart and spirit beyond the measure of most men, and his love for the Profile was profound.

Col. Greenleaf had engaged four men and a blacksmith to help me with the owrk. On the morning of September 25th, our labors began in earnest. A little after daylight we started up the mountain. Mr. Roberts was with us to be sure that we found our way, after leaving the mountain top, on the 800 foot descent to the top of the head. The turnbuckles had been taken apart so that the heaviest piece did not weigh over 25 pounds. The men were carrying pieces of the turnbuckles, and I about 30 pounds of tools. One man found the work too hard halfway to the top, two more reached the top, and two made the trip to the head. This was their first and last trip, with the exception of one man, who continued for three days. Every morning I carried some pieces so that by Sunday, October 1st, all the material was at the top.

I worked very hard that first day except for the times I was interrupted by the noise from automobile parties down at Profile Lake. I would stand on top of the forehead boulder and wave to them with a stick to which I tied a piece of white cloth. This happened many times during the day and the following days when it was clear enough for me to be seen. I worked as late as was safe, allowing only time enough to get off the mountain before dark. There being no trail from the top of the head to the mountain top, I had no desire to stay on the mountain all night.

There is nothing mechanical about the plan of fastening, and the only skill required was, first, to look out that you did not break your neck and, second, to drill a half lewis hole 11 inches deep, 5 inches wide on the inside, and 4 inches wide at the top, so that the half lewis would fit

Saving the Great Stone Face

exactly. Six holes were necessary to hold the three turnbuckles, three in the slipping boulder and three in the parent ledge. Two of these holes were drilled where I was obliged to stand on a shelf of rock 18 inches wide, and one slip would land me at the bottom of a precipice 260 feet below. No staging of any kind was used, as was reported in some newspaper accounts. Most of the time I had a rope about myself to prevent falling, for the wind blew in such squalls that I was forced to cling to the rope until it subsided. Some of the time rain fell in torrents — they told me it was the clouds striking the rocks as they swept through the Notch — but to me it felt like shower baths of ice water and I prefer to be excused from them in the late fall.

Wednesday night, September 27th, we had a very heavy rain and the next morning I was warned that it was not safe for any man to go up to the mountain. As my time was limited I decided to try it, for I had promised to be back on my job in Quincy in a week. Every narrow place on the trail was a raging torrent, and I was forced to leave the trail and climb among the trees or take a chance of being washed away in the opposite direction. About half way up the mountain, the trail began to get icy, but after many slips I reached the top. The cold was intense and my arms and legs were wet so that I began to suffer. When I looked down over those ice covered rocks, towards the head, I had an inclination to turn back.

It took all the courage I could muster to drive me down to the head. In many places I slid for 10 to 20 feet, which would have been all right if there was not the chance of going over the side of a big rock and falling 5 to 10 feet. If you missed what you aimed to fetch up against, where would you land? In eternity! But I reached the head and worked as hard as I could all day in frozen clothes! Perhaps some of you know how it feels. Two of my fingers were chilled so badly that one [of them] is now quite crooked. Coming back up [from the head] that night I was forced to cut places in the ice to climb on, and it certainly was a scary trip over those steep rocks. Snow had fallen in the afternoon and that made travelling more difficult. The weather continued very cold until Friday night, and no one would believe the amount of ice that formed in those two days. On Saturday there was a warm wind, the ice melted as quickly as it had formed, and when I returned that night, there was no snow or ice to be seen except on Mt. Lafayette, which must be two thousand feet higher than Profile Mountain.

Sunday was a beautiful day, and fearing the return of bad weather, I finished the half lewis holes, which so far had taken all my time. Each

First Repairs on the Profile

half lewis required three holes drilled with an inch and a quarter bit, so the hole would be an inch and a quarter in diameter and eleven inches deep. One hole is drilled on an angle of 20 degrees which makes the hole one inch wider at the bottom than at the top. Then the cores had to be broken out with a flat set, which was as hard as drilling two extra holes. That makes 55 inches of drilling to each half lewis hole. It is very hard work for one man to drill these holes, for such work is usually done by one man holding the drill and one or two others striking the drill with a heavy hammer. But, when the men Colonel Greenleaf had hired to help me all deserted, I did not intend to be beaten. I leave it to you to judge whether I had time to play or not.

On Monday, Mr. Roberts and Dr. Warden of Whitefield went up the mountain with me. I brimstoned the half lewises into the holes with their help. This was done to keep the water out of the holes, because if ice freezes in a flat hole it will split the stone, small or large, as quickly as powder. The turnbuckles were put in place and tightened and given a good coat of asphaltum varnish. Each of the turnbuckles is good for holding 70 tons and the forehead boulder is only 25 tons. This surplus of 185 tons is to resist the pressure of the ice and snow.

It took me eight days to do the work, twelve hours or a little more each day, working alone except for Monday, October 2nd, which was the shortest and easiest, and the warmest day. Just before painting the turnbuckles, I went down over the face, using three-quarter-inch rope fastened to a turnbuckle, and measured it from chin to forehead, a distance of 40 feet 5 inches. Mr. Roberts took several pictures of me down on the face, also several of the completed work.

It has frequently been stated that parts of the face have been chained or bolted on, but until I fastened the forehead boulder, no part of the Profile had ever been touched. I certainly would have seen any work had it ever been done. The work which I did is not visible either from the lake or highway viewing points.

After coming down the mountain, I was driven by team to Littleton, as the train had stopped running to the Profile House. I took the night train for Boston, arriving there the following morning rather weary and eight and one-half pounds lighter.

Before leaving the Profile House, Mr. Geddes told Colonel Greenleaf and Rev. Guy Roberts that the turnbuckles must be painted once a year to preserve and protect the steel from the ravages of the weather. If they were allowed to rust, serious trouble would result. How this continuing

Saving the Great Stone Face

care of the Old Man has been carried out is told in later chapters.

Concerning the cost of having that first repair work done, Mabelle explained:

I would like to state that there have been reports about the huge amount of money spent to rescue the Old Man. These reports are absolutely untrue. If the small amount [she doesn't say how much] received by my father for his work were to be printed here, it would be so ridiculous that no one would believe it. He risked his life to preserve the Old Man because he loved him and believed this to be too great a part of Nature's handiwork to be allowed to go to destruction.

The modest bill which Mr. Geddes sent for his work reached Colonel Greenleaf after he had been away for several weeks. The following letter, with a check, was received in October.

October 20, 1916

My dear Mr. Geddes:

I only returned last night from a trip West, so the delay in sending check for your bill. Please receipt bill and return to me at Hotel Vendome, Boston.

I wish to thank you for your kindness in coming to the Profile Hotel for the work required and for the able manner in which you performed the service.

With personal regards, I am,

Very truly yours,
C. H. Greenleaf

Late in December of the same year, Mr. Geddes received the following note from Governor Spaulding:

E. H. Geddes
21 Bedford St.
Quincy Mass.

Dear Sir:

I have received the handsome souvenir of the Old Man of the Mountain [no doubt a polished piece of granite] for which I thank you.

I am glad that the need of preserving this wonderful piece of Nature's

First Repairs on the Profile

handiwork was called to the attention of the State government during my administration and that we were able to get the matter attended to so thoroughly and well.

Yours very truly,
Roland H. Spaulding, Gov.

As for the durability of the Profile, it is appropriate to turn our attention to the sheer granite cliffs *behind* the Old Man. They drop steeply to slanting depths of rock fragments that have settled there as if dropped, chip by chip, from the chisel of a mighty Sculptor. With what great blows the Sculptor must have whittled away at the mountainside! Finally, with the stone fragments lying far below, the ledges in back of the Profile were removed, as if it had been planned that way, so the noble features could stand out, free and unobstructed, against the sky!

Mabelle wrote about these rocks:

In the fall, when the leaves are gone from the trees, the millions of fallen stones below the Old Man and for a distance of two miles to the south, can be seen piled one above the other. At the base of no other mountain in New England does this condition exist to such a noticeable extent. This shows that the profile was formed, not from anything that happened above it, but by the falling away of stones, as they were loosened, from either side and beneath it. Only the stones on ledges most firmly held to the parent rock remained.

In 1917, the year following the first repair work on the Profile, the name of the southern mountain slope where he resides was changed from Cannon to Profile in his honor. The change was made by the U.S. Geographic Board on March 7, 1917, on recommendation of J. W. Benedict, forest supervisor at Gorham, New Hampshire. The higher northern summit, still called Cannon Mountain, is named for the rock formation shaped like a cannon on an open ridge against the sky.

About this time, Rev. Guy Roberts was given a bronze medal by the Dartmouth Outing Club for his efforts to get the preservation work done on the Profile. The inscription recognized Roberts's services in "saving the face" of "The Old Man of the Mountain." This, the first award ever given by the Dartmouth Outing Club, was well deserved.

Saving the Great Stone Face

For some unknown reason, Edward Geddes never received an award or recognition for *his* work during his lifetime. It seems strange, for his skill and courage were of the noble mixture that makes heroes. Colonel Greenleaf said of him, "Mr. Geddes is deserving of much credit and praise for his knowledge of what should be done, and for his courage and ability in performing the work required. I think he has well earned State recognition."

However, it was not until the 1950s that recognition finally came to Geddes, and then because of the efforts of his daughter, Mabelle.* She possessed her father's determination for getting a worthwhile project done.

Thanks to Mabelle's unfaltering devotion, the wiry, indomitable man who had risked his life to save the Old Man, was at last given long-overdue acclaim. It came nearly forty years too late, unfortunately after he was gone. Thus are brave men, unsung in their lifetime, sometimes tardily given credit for great and unselfish deeds!

Edward Geddes never wanted praise or public honors. He was a quiet, purposeful man, dedicated to a cause, one who did not ask for reward beyond the simple payment for work well done. In his modesty he expressed the spirit of the noble face he came to love and know so intimately.

He would not be the last man to risk his life for the Profile. Several more brave men would follow, but Geddes was first, a pioneer in the risky, rewarding venture of saving the Great Stone Face.

*See Chapter 10.

First Repairs on the Profile

7

FOR SALE!
THE OLD MAN AND HIS NEIGHBORHOOD!

U NTIL the late 1920s, the Old Man and Franconia Notch remained, for worse or for better, in private ownership.

For worse was the "Outrage of 1893" when great swaths of valley and mountainside were denuded of trees and the road and stream were disfigured by a sawmill and several lumbermen's shanties. For better was the era of Taft and Greenleaf when the Flume and Notch hotels were in their heyday and when Geddes performed his protective "surgery" on the Great Stone Face.

Then came tragedy, a for sale sign, and a shocking threat to the entire Notch!

The second Flume House had burned in 1918 and was not rebuilt. In 1921, at the age of eighty, Colonel Greenleaf wished to retire from the hotel business. He sold his one remaining hotel, the Profile House with its beautiful community of twenty-nine cottages, stables, railroad station, and several thousand acres of forested valley and mountain slopes, including the Old Man, to Frank P. Abbott and Son (Karl) of nearby Bethlehem. The Abbotts already owned two attractive mountain hotels, the Forest Hills of Franconia, and the Uplands of Bethlehem. Colonel Greenleaf felt confident that his famous Franconia Notch resort, the Profile House, would continue to serve with great success its large and elite clientele for many years to come.

But the new ownership was to be brief.

Destruction of the Profile House

O N AUGUST 3, 1923, the entire complex of the Profile House went the way of so many White Mountain hotels. It was totally destroyed by fire. We can only imagine Colonel Greenleaf's dismay when word reached him in Pinehurst, New Jersey, that the hotel property he had known and loved for over sixty-five years was completely gone.

On that unhappy day the smoke could be seen for miles, belching upward in a dark column from between the mountain slopes that form Franconia Notch. In just a few hours, only smoldering ashes and stark blackened chimneys remained.

It was a beautiful August afternoon. As usual, the main house and cottages were crowded to capacity with guests, many of them longtime residents who had been returning for many summers to enjoy the comforts and attractions of this famous mountain resort.

Among the many clusters of relaxed vacationing guests, word was passed around that smoke had been seen coming out of the window of one of the bellboy's top floor bedrooms. The idea was disturbing, but there was no immediate concern. The resort had a good distribution of fire hoses, and there was an elaborate sprinkler system. Just to take proper precautions, however, the management announced that the supper meal would be delayed until the alarm could be checked out. Nobody doubted that it would be only a false report or, at the worst, only a localized blaze that could be quickly brought under control.

Like so many such tragedies, the source of the blaze was not found before it was too late to stop it, and then the cause really did not matter. Had the bellboy fallen asleep while smoking? Was defective electric wiring to blame? Had a kitchen accident sent a blaze up through the partitions? Who could ever be sure? At the time, what did it really matter? Only one fact was finally admitted — the hotel was on fire!

When the fearful reality was fully realized that the first tiny blaze had grown and was rapidly spreading, people scattered hurriedly to their rooms and cottages. They were soon intent on trying to save their possessions, although they still could not quite believe that tragedy had really struck.

The truth was already too evident at the powerhouse where the pump that governed the water supply had suddenly failed to function. Outside help was needed, fast! Telephone calls were hastily made to the fire departments of nearby towns. At best, it would take several precious minutes for even the nearest department at Franconia to climb Three Mile Hill and reach the rapidly spreading flames. There was nothing to do but to wait

For Sale!

The Profile House goes up in flames, August 2, 1923.

and try to rescue hotel records, personal belongings, and any valuable furnishings that could be carried.

As the *Littleton Courier* reported,

Of all the White Mountain resorts destroyed by fire, none was more tragic and complete than that of the Profile House. . . . If there had been sufficient water pressure, the property might have been saved. . . . Or had the blaze started on a lower floor, gravity pressure would have been sufficient at first, . . . but up under the roof the natural force was not enough. . . . In no time the main house was a roaring furnace.

There were many unsung heroes that day. Arriving along with the fire departments were truckloads of men, all volunteers anxious to help. One truck from Franconia brought my brother-in-law, Herman Fish, a master plumber who had been working on a local job. With his helpers and several other men picked up at Parker's general store, he raced his truck up the hill to the scene of destruction and helped haul out valuable furnishings and hastily packed trunks. The relatively safe nearby tennis courts were soon piled high with rescued belongings.

Nevertheless, many such efforts proved futile. Flying sparks were falling everywhere. Articles which seemed to be out of reach of the hungry flames were soon being consumed, and some possessions began to disappear — looters were at work! To meet this second danger police guards

Saving the Great Stone Face

The aftermath of the fire.

established roadblocks at each end of the hotel property and searched every car and truck leaving the scene. Several lots of valuable possessions were rescued.

Forest rangers and crews were stationed at the most exposed points of the surrounding forests. The natural draft through Franconia Notch could carry sparks far and wide. Fortunately, the woodlands were in no danger. The day before there had been a heavy rain, and the trees and ground were still damp. Otherwise, the whole of Franconia Notch might have become a roaring inferno. The thousands of acres of forests that make the old Man's neighborhood so beautiful and protect the Pemigewasset and other headwaters of the Merrimack River system could have been destroyed.

Fortunately, too, no one was seriously hurt. Of the more than 200 guests, about 275 employees, and an estimated 1,000 fire fighters and volunteer helpers, there were no casualties beyond scorched hands and faces, singed hair, and smoke-blackened clothes.

Within four hours, the twenty-six buildings of the beautiful Profile House community were flat. Only smoldering ruins remained, with here and there a lonely chimney to remind the weary and helpless onlookers of sheltering walls that had so suddenly and completely been destroyed.

The managers of several hotels in the surrounding mountain area hurried to the scene to offer at least temporary accommodations to the stunned and desolate guests, and positions to some of the now jobless employees.

For Sale!

Plowing the Notch in front of the present Tramway location in the early 1920s.

The whole region rallied to help the unfortunate, as usually happens in the first hours of tragedy.

At the time of the fire, the Abbotts were on their way home from a brief trip. They were located in New York and informed of the disaster. When they arrived the following day, they found only smoking ashes of what had been one of New England's most palatial and popular summer resorts.

During the next few days, one question was on everyone's mind: Would the owners rebuild?

The ruins were hardly cool when word went out that the owners would, indeed, build again. Son Karl, young, vigorous, and full of elaborate plans, assured everyone that a new Profile House would be ready for opening the following July 1. It would stand on the north shore of Profile Lake, in the very presence of the Old Man.

The many devotees of the Profile House received the good news with joy, but their hopes were soon to burst like a bubble. Son Karl changed his mind, and his highly esteemed father, Frank Abbott, was too elderly and frail to do what his son had decided not to do.

Then came the thunderbolt, striking without warning. The thousands

Saving the Great Stone Face

of acres of property surrounding the site of the Profile House were *for sale!* And that included the Great Stone Face!

The Fight to Save the Notch

THE NEXT MOVE was inevitable. Lumber companies rushed in to offer their bids for the vast expanse of valuable standing timber. The "Outrage of 1893" was to be repeated, but on a wholesale scale. Complete destruction of the forests now seemed imminent.

Words cannot begin to express the dismay of thousands of local residents and more thousands of visitors. The thought of Franconia Notch being stripped of its beautiful green forests was shocking. The Old Man's neighborhood would be ruined.

In the mid-1920s, throughout this struggle to prevent the demolition of the forests in the Notch, one organization with summer headquarters in Franconia played a leadership role. That was the Society for the Protection of New Hampshire Forests whose executive, Philip W. Ayres, devoted a major portion of his time and energy to this cause.* Although Ayres had earned a Ph.D. in history and economics at Johns Hopkins University and had served as director of the first school for social work in New York City, family considerations led him to reorient his career, and he became a trained forester. Thus, with him in the forefront of the fight to save New Hampshire's woodlands from the lumberman's ax, the society helped plan and coordinate the enormous efforts required to secure public ownership of this priceless treasure. The selling price of the Notch then under concessions to lumber companies was set at $400,000.

Although Governor John G. Winant had voiced some opposition to the price to members of the society's executive committee and was sufficiently disturbed to resign from that committee, the executive committee members voted to undertake the $400,000 fund-raising drive under Ayres's leadership. Later, Winant resolved his differences and strongly advocated passage of legislation for the state to appropriate $200,000 toward the project.

A Saturday feature article of about 2,500 words written by Allen Chamberlain appeared in the *Boston Transcript*. Introducing an interesting history of the Old Man and the Notch was the following timely paragraph:

---

*A plaque mounted on a rock by the sandy beach of Echo Lake reads: "1861-1945 In Memory of Philip Wheelock Ayres through whose vision and inspiring leadership the White Mountain National Forest and the Franconia Notch Reservation became the heritage of all the people."

For Sale!

The *"Boston Evening Transcript"* dramatized the battle to save the
Notch from the axe with this composite photograph.

Saving the Great Stone Face

Just as the people of the rest of the country, including even those of the Eastern States, have more than once gone to the rescue when any of those far Western scenic landmarks, such as the Yosemite or the Yellowstone, were in any way endangered, so now the country, even to the Pacific Coast, is showing an alert and helpful interest in New Hampshire's effort to place the far-famed Franconia Notch of the White Mountains beyond harm's way by putting it into public ownership. To every New Englander who has fared forth into other parts of the country, the Old Man of the Mountain stands as a symbol of the homeland. To every tourist from other sections who have visited the mountains, that massive granite visage is an indelible memory of the great White Hills. Old as the hills though it may be in fact, it has been known to white men at least, for scarcely more than a century, but once found by them it, and the beautiful mountain pass that it sentinels, soon gained a deserved fame as a beauty spot of high distinction. To preserve this property for public use will cost perhaps $400,000. With the hearty approval of Governor Winant, the Legislature has before it an appropriation bill carrying one-half of that sum, and the Society for the Protection of New Hampshire Forests proposes to raise the remainder.

The New Hampshire legislature rose to the challenge and appropriated the then enormous sum of $200,000 toward the purchase of the Notch in 1927. Mr. James J. Storrow of Boston, former treasurer of the society, made the unprecedented pledge of $100,000 toward the purchase. This left the sum of $100,000 to be raised by public subscription, with a deadline of June 1, 1928, when the purchase option would expire.

The drive was organized by the society with every expectation of success, and the response was splendid. Edward Tuck, a benefactor of a series of New Hampshire projects, including the Tuck School of Business Administration at Dartmouth College, responded to Ayres's appeal with a gift of $10,000. The Appalachian Mountain Club contributed over $7,000. Then Governor Huntley N. Spaulding personally contributed $1,000 together with untiring efforts for the program. The Federated Women's Clubs took to Ayers's idea of selling trees in the Notch to schoolchildren, clubs, and individuals all over the country for a dollar each.

Thanks to Nathaniel Hawthorne, frequent Granite State visitor, Franconia Notch had an appeal to those who might not otherwise identify with a society project. From Seattle, San Antonio, and points east, saving the Great Stone Face became the people's personal crusade. Many a newspaper from Maine to California had photographs of little boys on tricycles who

For Sale!

The Flume covered bridge, built around 1920, with Mount Flume in the background.

Saving the Great Stone Face

"owned" a tree in Franconia Notch. Schoolchildren contributed dimes and quarters to the cause. The *Manchester Union* solicited funds zealously.

Other individuals and organizations made significant contributions. Important among these were numerous garden clubs. Thus, the valuable 6,000 acres stretching along seven miles of the Daniel Webster Highway and reaching up the mountain slopes to include the Old Man were saved by state appropriation, large contributions, and over 15,000 individual contributions!

Once the new ownership was established, Governor Huntley N. Spaulding joined with the state forestry commission and the Society for the Protection of New Hampshire Forests in obtaining the services of Arthur A. Shurcliff, a landscape architect. He was directed to reestablish the Notch, especially the parts already disturbed, to its primeval beauty, with the intention of making the entire area a memorial park.

The upper five sixths of the Notch was to be immediately placed under the control of the state. It was determined that it would be wise for the society to hold and run the Flume for twenty years before releasing that portion of the Notch to the state for administration. The funds raised would be used for trail building and related beautification programs as a whole. C. T. Bodwell, who had worked for the society at the Lost River Reservation, was appointed director and for the next twenty years carried on a splendid management and development job for the property.

Probably because of the widening public interest in the fate of Franconia Notch, the road through the valley was at last opened for winter travel in the fall of 1928. In 1926 the Littleton Chamber of Commerce, together with the chambers of Lisbon, Franconia, Bethlehem, Whitefield, and other North Country towns, tried to start definite action to keep the Notch road open, but nothing was accomplished. Finally, in October 1927, the *Littleton Courier* carried this welcome announcement: "On Monday the Governor and Council voted to have the State Highway keep the Notch road open. Special plows will be ready as soon as snow begins to fall. Now travelers and visitors can see the beauty of the Notch in winter."

The Notch purchase was dedicated on September 15, 1928, to the men and women of New Hampshire who had served the nation in time of war. Another great crisis had been met. It would not be the last one in the dramatic history of Franconia Notch and the Great Stone Face, but it was one more important step in the wise control of their destiny.

For Sale!

Profile Lake
Edward Hill, date unknown
18" x 14"
Oil on canvas
Collection: New Hampshire Historical Society

Honors
for
the Old Man

FTER THE FRANTIC but successful race against time to secure a program of public ownership for the Notch, some twenty years of comparative calm and safety followed. The postwar period was marked by rising national prosperity. This was reflected by increasing numbers of tourists visiting Franconia Notch and the Old Man of the Mountain as New Hampshire improved her roads and her scenic wonders became even better known. In 1955 the Profile observed its 150th anniversary birthday, and President Eisenhower honored the occasion as he paid tribute to the Old Man during his whirlwind tour of the state. In this same period belated honors were paid to two men who had been instrumental in preserving the Profile.

It was a good time for America, a good time for the Old Man and for Franconia Notch, but it would not be long before action would be needed to preserve the Notch once again, this time from development of a four-lane major highway through its narrow corridor.

8

DEDICATION AND CONTROVERSY

THE DEDICATION of Franconia Notch as a state park, and the adoption of a state emblem, were seventeen years apart, but both of these important events focused attention on the Great Stone Face. The Notch dedication in 1928 was held on the shore of Profile Lake within the area that is best for viewing the Old Man, and his likeness was chosen in 1945 to be placed in the oval center of New Hampshire's state emblem.

Notch Dedication, September 15, 1928

ON SATURDAY afternoon, September 15, 1928, Franconia Notch was officially dedicated as a "State Forest Reservation and Park," to be a memorial forever honoring the men and women of New Hampshire who served the nation in times of war.

I attended the dedication and took part in it. For very personal reasons, which I soon will relate, I was greatly impressed and deeply thrilled.

Chapter 260

Joint Resolution authorizing the governor and council to dedicate the Franconia Notch Forest Reservation and State Park as a Memorial to the Men and Women of New Hampshire who have served the Nation in times of war.

Moving the memorial boulder from the roadside in the Notch to the head of Profile Lake.

Resolved by the Senate and House of Representatives in General Court convened:

That, upon the acquisition by the state of the title to the Franconia Notch, under the terms of the act approved April 21, 1925, the governor and council be and they hereby are authorized and directed to dedicate the forest reservation and state park contemplated by said act as a memorial to the men and women of New Hampshire who have served the nation in times of war.

Approved April 30, 1928.

The dedication program was described in detail in the following week's issue of the *Littleton Courier*. Excerpts from that article follow:

NOTCH RESERVATION IS FORMALLY DEDICATED

The Old Man of the Mountains beheld a very noble ceremony enacted on the shore of gem-like Profile Lake Saturday afternoon. It was the unveiling of a tablet officially opening Franconia Notch as a memorial park and forest reservation. The tablet, imbedded in the face of a huge boulder,

Saving the Great Stone Face

which is composed of the same quality granite from which nature carved The Great Stone Face, and located at the head of Profile Lake, about 75 feet west of the highway, was unveiled by Governor Huntley N. Spaulding.

The bronze tablet, which is placed upon the sloping side of a huge glacial boulder [Commemoration Rock] which at one time was no doubt a part of the rocky summit of some nearby peak, carries the following inscription: "Franconia Notch Reservation and Memorial Park, acquired with funds appropriated by the Legislature of 1925 and the donations of 15,000 contributors, secured through the Society for the Protection of New Hampshire Forests, dedicated as a Memorial to the men and women of New Hampshire who served the nation in times of war. September 1928."

The exercises were brief, lasting only an hour, but into that short time was crowded a program of unusual merit, in which some of the state's most distinguished citizens participated. Former Governor John G. Winant, in whose administration the bill was passed, making it possible to acquire Franconia Notch, was the first speaker. He told the gathering of the action of the 1925 Legislature in passing the bill which provided an appropriation of $200,000 toward the purchase of the Notch. Although the actual deal was not consummated during his administration, it was this law which made it possible for negotiations to be carried on.

W. R. Brown, chairman of the State Forestry Commission, presided, and after the talk by Governor Winant, introduced Allen Hollis, president of the Society for the Protection of New Hampshire Forests. Mr. Hollis told how the Society's efforts during the past five years made possible the exercises of Saturday. Mrs. George F. Morris, president of the State Federation of Women's Clubs, related the activities of that organization in connection with the campaign to raise money to purchase the Notch. The women did a wonderful work and to them should go much of the credit for the acquiring of the needed funds.

Governor Spaulding officially unveiled the tablet and said in part: "These ceremonies stand for the final success of long continued efforts to bring these natural wonders of world-wide fame, Franconia Notch and the Profile, within public ownership and control."

Judge James W. Remick of Littleton made a stirring speech of acceptance.

Following the unveiling of the tablet, a color guard and buglers from Riley Strong Post of the American Legion in Littleton added impressiveness to the ceremony. Throughout the afternoon, the 172nd Field Artillery Band of Manchester entertained with martial music, and as a concluding feature

Dedication and Controversy

The band on the shore of Profile Lake during the dedication ceremonies.

musical numbers from the pageant "Woodland" depicting saving of Franconia Notch were presented by pupils from the Kilburn school in Littleton. Frances Johnson had this in charge and wrote the pageant.

As the *Courier* article related, the afternoon of the dedication was cold and cloudy. During the hour-long program, shifting clouds allowed only partial glimpses of the Profile. Then came the closing feature, my Kilburn School pupils singing songs from my pageant, "Woodland," and my "Old Man of the Mountains." The children were in two groups. One group dressed in blue crepe paper costumes to represent the clear waters of Franconia Notch lakes and streams; the other group dressed in green crepe paper costumes to represent the forests that had been saved from the lumber companies.

As the children stood at the edge of Profile Lake, singing and looking up at the mostly hidden Profile, I felt keen disappointment that he had not fully appeared. I was standing at the edge of the crowd where I could, without being conspicuous, direct the singers. Suddenly, as they began the chorus "Old Man of the Mountains, Proud, noble, supreme," a miracle happened. The wind swept aside the tumbling clouds, and the Old Man came into full, clear view. Then, as the song ended, clouds again veiled

Saving the Great Stone Face

Scene from the pageant "Woodland" which concluded the ceremonies.

the Great Stone Face. It was as though he had recognized the tribute of little children.

Everyone present was hushed and, I am sure, deeply stirred. My eyes were blurred with tears, and my heart was full of gratitude. It had been a rare and beautiful moment!

According to mutual agreement, the Society for the Protection of New Hampshire Forests was to own and control the southernmost 1,000 acres, including the Flume and the Pool, while the state has title to the remaining 5,000 acres at the north, including the Great Stone Face. The intent was that the society would deed its portion of the land to the state in twenty years, which it did on December 31, 1948.

The first director of the Flume end of the Notch was Clare ("Tom") Bodwell. A more dedicated, enthusiastic man could not have been found. Tom was born in Riverton, Nebraska, but came with his family, at the age of six, to Bethlehem, New Hampshire. He married a Bethlehem woman, Inez E. Whitcomb, and had two daughters, Natalie and Lucille. When he was appointed director of the Flume Reservation, the family moved to Franconia. Always deeply concerned about conservation and forest management, Tom believed strongly with Dr. Charles Eliot that "to establish a forest reservation is as nearly immortal as any human ef-

Dedication and Controversy

fort can be; it is self-perpetuating and lasts from generation to generation." With glowing energy and devotion, Tom applied this belief to the expanded management of the Flume Reservation for many years. He also developed a deep love for the Old Man and his preservation. On one trip to the Profile, accompanied by his daughter Lucille's husband, G. Peter Macon, he told the younger man, "Please scatter my ashes here." Peter remembered, and when Tom passed away in February 1976, Peter carried out the wish. On a lovely August day of that year he took the ashes of that devoted friend of the Old Man and, with the permission of the Notch management, scattered them among the weathered rocks of the Old Man's forehead.

After the dedication and during the next seventeen years before the adoption of a state emblem in 1945, the Old Man witnessed many developments in his neighborhood.

The "Use but Not Abuse" Controversy

IN SPITE of the Notch's protected status, the question of *how* to preserve it was still an issue. National fame brought more and more tourists to visit the Old Man, and both the state and the Society for the Protection of New Hampshire Forests were faced with finding adequate means of accommodating them. By this time the automobile had become the major mode of transportation to the Notch, adding a further complication to park management.

The conflict between preservation and recreation, so important in Notch development, had already been pointed out by Judge James Remick in his speech at the dedication ceremonies in 1928: "If we would make this Memorial Park more and more worthy of the men and women to whom it has been here dedicated . . . we shall remove the last vestige of commercialism and every contrivance of men which now mars its beauty and grandeur and lessens its appeal to the soul, and ever after safeguard it as God made it."

This view, echoed by others who wanted to return Franconia Notch State Park to a natural state, was related in the "Franconia Notch State Park Plan" of 1977.

In 1929 the Society hired a landscape architect and frequent Notch visitor, Arthur Shurcliff, to prepare plans for development. He met with the State Forestry Commission, the Society, the Highway Department, and other concerned citizens to discuss immediate and long-range plan-

Saving the Great Stone Face

ning objectives. At this time, the roadside and its relation to the Park was under the general control of the Forestry Commission. It was not until 1940 that the State Highway Department gained control over all the highway passing through the state reservation.

Mr. Shurcliff's recommendations emphasized the purposes for which Franconia Notch State Park had been acquired: to preserve Franconia Notch as a public reservation and memorial park. Under his guidance, it was decided that certain special services should be provided, including limited camping, picnic, parking and sanitary facilities; and that these facilities should be located near the major attractions but well off the main road and as inconspicuous as possible. Special attention was given to highway improvements along the eastern shore of Echo Lake to assure a minimum of cutting and filling. The first real improvement work began in 1929 when the site of the old Profile House was reforested.

The early 30s witnessed further efforts to clean up the remains of commercial interests in the Notch. Many of the park buildings that exist today were constructed during this period with assistance from the Civilian Conservation Corps. At the same time, the Society was improving facilities at the Flume and making long-range plans for the future.

However, the plan to remove commercialism from the Park was being challenged at the north end of Franconia Notch where an aerial tramway for skiers was proposed in 1935. Skiing interests in Franconia Notch began in the early 30s as enthusiasm for the sport began to spread throughout the White Mountains. With the help of the CCC's, the Richard Taft Trail on Cannon Mountain was built in 1932 and became the first racing trail in the country. Soon afterwards, ski enthusiasts began to agitate for a ski lift. As a result, an aerial tramway was proposed for Cannon Mountain, directly back of the Great Stone Face.

An effort was made in the 1935 Session of the Legislature to authorize construction of the Tram, but these efforts did not materialize. Initially, the Society for the Protection of New Hampshire Forests registered a protest, but withdrew its objections after it was agreed that all Tramway developments would be subject to approval by what was now the State Forestry and Recreation Commission. In 1937, a legislative act established an Aerial Tramway Commission and authorized a bond issue of $250,000. Tramway construction was completed in 1938. It was the first in a series of major steps leading to the intensive development of ski trails, slopes, parking areas, and other facilities which we see today.

On June 28, 1938, dedication ceremonies were held at the Tramway

Dedication and Controversy

Cleaning up the landslide of September 21, 1938.

Valley Station. Nearly 1,000 people, including state and federal officials, listened to the program sent out over an amplifying system from the tram car waiting at the base of the mountain. Governor Francis P. Murphy dedicated the Tramway "to the service and the great good of the people of New Hampshire and the happy use and enjoyment of all." The governor's wife christened the car with a bottle of water from nearby Echo Lake and named the cars the *Lafayette* and the *Lincoln* for the two peaks on the east side of the Notch. Then the first carload of invited guests was taken up the mountain, and the Tramway was officially ready to serve the public.

For the next eleven and a half years, the actual operation of this famous White Mountain attraction was under the personal and able direction of Roland Peabody, who had worked so vigorously to make the Tramway a reality. He became a familiar figure to the many visitors returning every season because the Tramway was his special joy and concern. His friendly greeting, keen wit, and tireless devotion to the area he loved made him a favorite everywhere he went. The Tramway grew and became widely known under his leadership. By its tenth birthday nearly 1.25 million passengers had been carried to the mountaintop. It was a four-season mecca for people from all over the world.

As further noted by the "Franconia Notch State Park Plan" of 1977,

Saving the Great Stone Face

A fundamental reshaping of management goals had been taking place since 1928. Certainly, the advice of Judge Remick and the recommendations of Mr. Shurcliff had received short shrift in the development of Cannon Mountain, as illustrated by Shurcliff's correspondence to the State Forester in 1941: "Recently when passing through Franconia Notch, I found myself thinking over the ideals which were discussed for its preservation. . . . It was plain that these ideals were based on the belief that the natural beauty of the Notch must be preserved . . . that no new blemishes would be made and that no recreative facility would compete by extent or prominence with the scenic beauty of the Notch. . . . Any effort to make a concession or a utility a source of income beyond the normal and relatively small requirements of visitors, would jeopardize the very purpose for which the Notch was acquired, and would threaten public confidence in the custody of the State."

In September 1940 Governor Murphy and the Executive Council granted the State Highway Department control over all the highways passing through the state reservations. That, of course, included Franconia Notch, and would lead to the long and heated I-93 controversy.

In 1941 the League of New Hampshire Craftsmen was given a concession to remodel and utilize the old railroad station of former Profile House days as a museum salesroom and workshop. This arrangement continued until the league outlet was moved to "Ernie's Haus" on the west side of Echo Lake.*

Also in 1941, the governor requested a study of Franconia Notch State Park by the State Planning and Development Commission. This report focused on the fact that a total of eight separate agencies were operating facilities and contributing to park development. The commission recommended consolidation of all facilities under one administration and development of a master plan to give the park a unified character and provide unified services. The commission also recommended that all man-made services be designed to permit preservation of the Notch's natural features.

War broke out and nothing further was done until five years later, when the Society deeded its 1,000 acres to the state. W. R. Brown, chairman of the Forestry and Recreation Commission, indicated the management philosophy the state had adopted for Franconia Notch in his dedication speech when he said, in part:

*The building was given in memory of their son by the Glaessel family.

Dedication and Controversy

The Tramway in 1939, its first year of operation.

Saving the Great Stone Face

As to the general policy of operation of Franconia Notch Area, there appear to be two conflicting views that have received publicity. From the ultra-conservative standpoint, the scenic splendor of this popular area should be preserved as a sylvan wilderness, where only quiet and solitude should prevail and the minimum of provision made for the public. From the other extreme standpoint, this area should be developed with a view towards receiving the greatest possible revenue from the greatest number of people even at the expense of some of its natural wildness.

Our Commission believes in the middle way between these extremes, signified by the expression "Use but not Abuse." It is confident that Franconia Notch's wilderness splendor can be preserved by the careful protection of its natural scenery, and at the same time, by good planning, the comfort of myriads of nature lovers, who will pour through this Notch, can be provided for. The inspiration derived from a trip through the White Mountains is not alone for the young, the strong or the privileged few, it is equally appreciated by the old, the weak, or the underprivileged dwellers in our hot cities. The cult of exclusiveness can be no part of a public trust, and all the people who come to enjoy our beautiful State must be hospitably received, albeit with reasonable restrictions for the general good.

And so the controversy over how to develop Franconia Notch went on with the different interest groups striving to gain control. It was the old and ever present conflict between conservation and so-called progress, a battle that would continue to recur in various forms.

Meanwhile, New Hampshire was looking for a suitable design for a state emblem.

Our State Emblem

OUR NEW HAMPSHIRE state seal bore the picture of an unfinished ship in the process of construction, appropriate for an original colony and state where shipbuilding had been a leading industry. But by 1945 New Hampshire had a variety of industries, and her interior, especially her White Mountains region, was gaining national and even international attention as a year-round resort area. The 150th anniversary of the discovery of the Old Man of the Mountain was only ten years away, and Franconia Notch had already become a skiers' mecca since the Tramway was built in 1938.

When discussions began over choosing a design for an emblem, attention was already focused on Franconia Notch and the Great Stone Face. It was natural that the Profile should gain favor in considering a design.

In fact, the Old Man was such a timely subject that it was suggested he appear with the ship on the state seal. On January 18, 1945, Harry P. Smart of Ossipee introduced House Joint Resolution 9 providing for a committee to study and draw up a design for a state seal.

On January 24, 1945, the house judiciary committee reported house joint resolution 9 "inexpedient to legislate"; next it was reconsidered and passed; then on March 22 the senate judiciary committee also reported the resolution "inexpedient," and it was killed. General opinion held that a new emblem would be too expensive and involve too much inconvenience in changing the seal on all official papers, documents, and so forth. Several weeks elapsed until house bill 288, which was introduced by Laurence Pickett of Keene for the committee on rules on April 10, 1945, was enacted into law. The act described the new emblem as follows:

The state emblem shall be of the following design: Within an elliptical panel, the longest dimension of which shall be vertical, there shall appear an appropriate replica of the Old Man of the Mountains surrounding the inner panel, and enclosed within another ellipse, there shall be at the top of the design the words of any state motto which may be adopted by the general court; and, at the bottom of the design, between the inner and outer elliptical panels, the words, "New Hampshire" appropriately separated from the motto, if adopted, by one star on each side. Said emblem may be placed on all printed or related material issued by the state and its subdivisions relative to the development of recreational, industrial, and agricultural resources of the State.

In 1957 the act was amended to reverse the position of the designations "New Hampshire" and "Live Free or Die," the state name being placed at the top. The brave words were said to have been shouted by Gen. John Stark, New Hampshire's great Revolutionary War hero, during one of the battles of that struggle for American freedom. He knew so well that a person dies in spirit if he is not free!

State Ownership

IN 1947, two years after the adoption of our state emblem, the Society for the Protection of New Hampshire Forests deeded its 1,000 acres to the state, and the entire 6,000 acres of Franconia Notch became state property under the direction of Russell B. Tobey, veteran director of the state division of parks.

Although many years of controversy would follow over how to manage the Notch, important steps had been taken to preserve it. The beautiful forests had been saved from lumber companies, and the Notch, including the Old Man, had been transferred to state ownership and dedicated as a memorial park.

*The state emblem adopted in 1945
featuring the Old Man.*

Dedication and Controversy

9

THE PROFILE'S 150TH BIRTHDAY

T HE PROFILE is, of course, a very Old Man. He is much older than can be measured by any human reckoning of time, but 1955 marked a very special year in his long life story. It was the 150th anniversary of his discovery by white men in 1805. A celebration of the historic event focused worldwide attention on this unique natural wonder. Several months of preparation and publicity preceded the anniversary celebration which was observed June 24, 1955.

Special attention was drawn to the profile in December 1951 when *New Hampshire Profiles* published its first issue. The frontispiece was a fine photograph of the Profile, and under it was a poem of mine.

The *Littleton Courier* suggested several ideas for celebrating the 150th birthday in its issue of April 8, 1954. Excerpts from the editorial follow.

New Hampshire's world-famous landmark, the Old Man of the Mountains, will have an important birthday next year, for 1955 will mark the sesquicentennial of the discovery of the Great Stone Face in Franconia Notch by white men.

In the 150th anniversary lies a golden opportunity for New Hampshire to stage a celebration that will not only fittingly observe the occasion, but also serve to focus national attention on the many advantages of this countryside as a vacation-land. The occasion seems to be tailor-made for publicity and promotion and, properly organized and conducted, could prove a real magnet to draw increasing thousands of visitors to our state

90

in 1955. *The Courier believes this suggestion will find ready response on the part of everyone, not only those who live near Franconia Notch but in all other parts of the state.*

We believe that many ideas that have been brought forth in past years about how best to attract and keep more and more visitors here longer, could be utilized in making New Hampshire, and especially the area around the Old Man, appeal to the vacationist who is looking not only for scenic beauty and wonders of nature but also for things to do while on his vacation.

Through the cooperation of the governor and all state agencies, the regional and area organizations, and all local Chambers of Commerce and other civic groups, the Granite State could stage a bang-up celebration in 1955. The Courier hereby pledges its full support of such a project. Advance copies of this editorial have been sent to Governor Hugh Gregg, Russell Tobey, recreation director of the New Hampshire Forestry and Recreation Department (under whose direction Franconia Notch is operated), This Is New Hampshire, Inc. and the State Planning and Development Commission, our two state-wide organizations, the White Mountains Region Association, and the Littleton Chamber of Commerce.

If the idea takes hold, the planning and operation of such an anniversary celebration might well be in the hands of a general state committee, representing various parts of the state. We are sure that there are plenty of capable individuals in the North Country who would be willing to do their share in such work, along with folks from other sections of New Hampshire.

Preparations for the Party

THE *Littleton Courier* continued to report on the plans for the anniversary in its July 1, 1954, issue.

The first step in promoting the year 1955 as "New Hampshire's Vacation Jubilee" was taken this week, when Governor Hugh Gregg announced the appointment of George T. Noyes, well known Bethlehem insurance man, as chairman of a statewide committee to be in charge of the summertime celebration next year that will headline the observance of the 150th anniversary of the discovery of the Old Man of the Mountains by white men, and similar historical events in other parts of the Granite State.

From the first, Governor Gregg has been enthusiastic, and he is expected to announce his appointments of the complete general committee in the

The Profile's 150th Birthday

near future. On Tuesday night at the annual meeting of the Monadnock Region Association, in Peterborough, he made his first public announcement of the preliminary plans, and stated that his first committee appointee was Major A. Erland Goyette of Peterborough. Other names will be announced as appointments are made.

One of the preanniversary activities involved the famous Bretton Woods Boy Singers who sang my song, "Old Man of the Mountains," on many occasions. It came about because one day in June 1954 Frank R. Hancock (better known as "Uncle Frank"), who had founded the group in 1910 and continued as its director since that time, was at the *Courier* office making arrangements with my good friend, Reg Colby, to have the Boy Singers' summer concert schedule printed. Reg suggested that my Old Man song would be an appropriate number for the concerts that summer and gave Uncle Frank a copy. Frank not only liked the song and the idea but made a special arrangement which the boys sang at more than twenty concerts that summer.

The first concert of the season was given at the historic Crawford House (destroyed by fire in November 1977) situated at the head of Crawford Notch. Reg and his wife Peg invited me to accompany them to the opening concert. After the program, Reg introduced me to Uncle Frank. Before I could express my deep appreciation of the Boy Singers' beautiful rendition, Uncle Frank inquired in his gay, buoyant manner, "Well, how did you like the way we tore your song apart?" (Those were his first words to his future wife — whom he married in 1961!).

Since the copyright of my Old Man song was about to run out, as my first contribution to the anniversary I had a new edition printed in time for the Old Man's 150th birthday.

Next I inquired of Houghton Mifflin Company regarding the copyright of their publication, Nathaniel Hawthorne's "The Legend of the Great Stone Face." When I learned that the famous legend was in the public domain, I arranged to have a new edition printed by the Courier Printing Company.

A third anniversary project of mine was producing a giant postcard. The card showed a close-up photograph of the Old Man, and beside it my "Great Stone Face" poem.

Because the celebration meant so much to me, I was greatly thrilled when I learned that the Bretton Woods Boy Singers had been invited to sing my Old Man song at the birthday celebration. My excitement was beyond anything I can express when I was invited to ride with the Boy Singers to the historic event and sit with them on the canopied platform

Saving the Great Stone Face

where the ceremonies were to take place. We would be in the select group which included President Eisenhower, several national and state dignitaries, and a formidable bodyguard of policemen.

I was *not* thrilled, but deeply concerned, when I heard of talk to illuminate the Old Man at night. I immediately wrote a letter of protest in response to a vote of opinions being taken by *New Hampshire Profiles.* *

When an attempt to use powerful searchlights was tried, and proved impractical, I was one of many loyal friends of the Old Man who felt great gratitude that the publicity stunt had to be abandoned. More dignified plans, worthy of the Profile, were now nearly ready for fulfillment, one of the most noteworthy being a commemorative stamp.

Mabelle Geddes Russell told something about the anniversary in her book.

Throughout the State a wide variety of events had been scheduled to take place during the summer months of 1955. The 150th birthday of the Old Man of the Mountains was the center of all the plans. Two events of major importance were scheduled. On Tuesday, June 21, a special pro-

*The author's three principal objections were: artificial light would be unnecessarily expensive; spotlights would lend an artificial atmosphere to a natural wonder; and the Old Man can be seen at night without illumination, even on a dark night when his face is dimly visible. The full text of the letter is reproduced in the appendices. Ed.

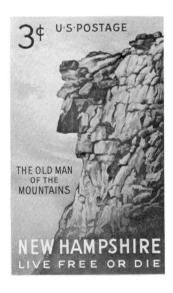

Facsimile of the Old Man commemorative stamp issued June 21, 1955.

The Profile's 150th Birthday

Pine tree chin wiskers for the Old Man, put in place by ingenous and daring Dartmouth undergraduates just before President Eisenhower's visit, lasted only hours after being discovered.

gram was held in Franconia, from 10 A.M. to noon, to celebrate the First Day of Issue of the Old Man of the Mountains commemorative stamp. On Friday, June 24, at 9 A.M. in the Notch, a Birthday Party was staged with President Eisenhower as the guest of honor.

The commemorative stamp was the first ever to be issued to the State of New Hampshire. I think by now everyone has seen the stamp, the central design being the profile view of the Old Man.

The historic outdoor [commemorative] program at the combination Franconia town hall and post office was dignified and impressive. The weather was warm and sunny. Governor Lane Dwinell, U.S. Senator Norris Cotton, U.S. Representative Perkins Bass, and Assistant U.S. Postmaster General Albert J. Robertson, were on hand for the exercises. Master of Ceremonies was Philip Cole of Franconia.

The program included music by McLure's Student Band [of Litteton], invocation and benediction were by Reverend Esther Vodola of Church of Christ, Franconia, welcome [was] by Reginald M. Colby of [the] Littleton [Courier], and remarks [were] by the several guests. Congressman Bass, the final speaker, paid tribute to Rev. Guy Roberts and Edward H.

Saving the Great Stone Face

Geddes [Mabelle's father], without whose services it is quite possible that there would not have been an Old Man to have a celebration for.

The Birthday, June 24, 1955

I SHOULD LIKE TO QUOTE Mabelle Geddes once again.

The Birthday Party was held at the Cannon Mt. Tramway parking area. It was impossible to hold it within sight of the Old Man because of lack of ample space. At the southern end of the parking area is a natural rise of land on which was built a canopied stand for the presentation of the Historical Pageant, President Eisenhower's address, and other highlights of the program. Facing this stand, about 5,000 chairs were placed in the parking area. The weather was partly cloudy with the sun breaking through at times. George T. Noyes of Bethlehem was Chairman of the Birthday Party program. Among those in the presidential party were Governor Lane Dwinell, U.S. Senators Styles Bridges and Norris Cotton, Congressmen Chester Merrow and Perkins Bass, Assistant to the President Sherman Adams, and White House Press Secretary James Hagerty.

An attractive four-page commemorative program folder was distributed to all who attended the birthday celebration. I have used the program, the largest issue of the *Littleton Courier* in its sixty-six-year history, and my recollections of the highlights of the great day for this book.

For me, of course, it was a day of special excitement. I drove over to Twin Mountain where I had left my car and met the bus carrying Uncle Frank and the Bretton Woods Boy Singers. An open pickup truck had gone ahead with the piano and the accompanist, Robert K. Love. When we arrived at the scene of events, they, the piano, and Mr. Love were already established behind a screen of young trees in back of the canopied platform. There was room for about fifty people on the platform, and all of us were given special commemorative badges to indicate that we had a right to be there. The singers group and I had seats at the rear of the platform so that the boys could easily line up across the back and near the concealed piano to sing my Old Man song. As we took our places there was an air of suspense in the audience facing the platform, and also among the special guests already gathered on the dais. There would be about two hours of events before President Eisenhower's arrival, but everything seemed geared to that important part of the program, all of

The Profile's 150th Birthday

which was under the direction of Chairman George T. Noyes.

In "the midst of mountain splendor," with the man of the hour, the Great Stone Face, just out of sight on high cliffs of Profile Mountain at the left of the crowds as they faced the platform, the three-hour program began at nine o'clock that morning. The invocation by the Reverend Frank W. Cole, rector of St. Luke's Church in Woodsville, was followed by an hour's concert of stirring music by the 100-piece U.S. Army Field Band from Fort George Meade, Maryland, under the direction of Maj. Chester E. Whiting.

Following the band concert, a colorful twelve-scene Franconia Notch Historical Pageant was presented. It was written by Enzo Serafini of Sugar Hill and was directed by Mrs. Curtis H. Brockelman of Franconia. As the scenes were enacted, Seri delivered the commentary.

At the close of the pageant Chairman Noyes introduced me to the audience as composer of the "Old Man of the Mountains" song which the Bretton Woods Boy Singers would present later in the program. He then introduced Enzo Serafini as author and narrator of the pageant.

After the introductions, the band played for about a half hour while waiting for President Eisenhower to arrive in his swiftly moving motorcade.

Meanwhile, coming north by way of Concord, New Hampshire's capital, the presidential party was making two stops. One was at Lincoln, home of Sherman Adams, and the other was at the Profile. A temporary platform with railing had been built at the place where the Old Man is best seen, and here President Eisenhower and his party stood for a few minutes while he looked up for the first time at the Great Stone Face. Then the motorcade continued north to the upper end of Franconia Notch where his appearance was awaited.

Suddenly there was a burst of excitement as the cars swung into the heavily guarded area behind the platform. The presidential party had arrived. All at once there were military guards everywhere. We were cautioned to remain in our seats to prevent any undue commotion, as the president of the United States and his party strode from their cars to the back of the platform, then down the center aisle to their front-row seats at each side of the speaker's stand.

The president was introduced by Senator Cotton and received by the large throng with enthusiastic and friendly clapping and cheering.

Following are the opening lines of the president's speech:

Governor Dwinell, Members of the New Hampshire Congressional delegation, distinguished guests, and my fellow Americans:

Saving the Great Stone Face

Only a few moments ago, I had the first opportunity of my life to look at the Old Man of the Mountains. The natural question asked me was, "What did you think of it, Mr. President?" I answered, as anyone would in polite conversation and said, "Remarkable. Wonderful. Interesting."

*The real thought that crossed my mind was: "What does the Old Man of the Mountains think of us?"**

Following the president's speech, Governor Dwinell presented him with a silver bowl and ladle bearing a facsimile of the Old Man of the Mountain, a gift from the state of New Hampshire. Then Chairman Noyes gave him a commemorative stamp album containing the Old Man stamp which had been issued three days earlier at the Franconia post office.

After the presentations the Bretton Woods Boy Singers sang my Old Man song, accompanied by Mr. Love at the concealed piano. The boys were lined up across the back of the platform, with Uncle Frank directing. Following the piano introduction the well-trained young voices sent forth the song in rich, clear tones, to echo among the mountains from the many loudspeakers and go out over the air by radio. I was thrilled, of course, and felt sure that the Old Man was listening. It was the second important occasion at which my song had been sung to him.

*The president linked the Old Man's hopes to those of the world, "peace on earth, good will to men." The complete text of the speech will be found in the appendices. Ed.

President Eisenhower addresses the crowd at the birthday celebration.

The Profile's 150th Birthday

A smiling president greets a young admirer as he leaves the speaker's platform. Press Secretary James Hagarty is at the left.

During the song President Eisenhower and the other special guests on the front row turned around to watch and listen. The president, his face beaming with appreciation, never took his eyes from the singers. Following the benediction, he shook hands with each boy, a rare privilege for them. Later, on television, they sang the Old Man song on top of Mount Washington as channel 8's signing-off number.

Crowds lined both sides of the highway to wave and cheer as the motorcade sped toward Whitefield, Lancaster, and Berlin, on a brief overnight tour of New Hampshire's North Country. At Whitefield the president stopped at the Mountain View Hotel, where he was given a copy of my Old Man song.

In connection with the birthday party for the Old Man, Franconia held a homecoming observance on July 2, 3, and 4. A handsome brochure included historical information and pictures, together with four pages about the Old Man which they proudly called "Our Leading Citizen." At the bottom of the last page was an interesting perforation made with a ticket

Saving the Great Stone Face

punch used by Charles Whipple, a conductor on the railroad that ran into the Notch. He was the father of Mrs. Roland E. Peabody of Franconia. This is believed to be the only such punch in existence. The perforation was a good, though small likeness of the Great Stone Face.

Thus closed the colorful and dramatic 150th birthday celebration! It was an event of historical importance, an occasion never to be forgotten.

The Profile's 150th Birthday

10

HONORS FOR ROBERTS AND GEDDES

I T WAS UNFORTUNATE that state recognition did not come to Roberts and Geddes until several years after they had died. Their combined efforts had prolonged the life of the Old Man and had started legislative action for a regular schedule of inspection and any necessary repair· work. Yet these two modest men, heroes in purpose and achievement, went unrecognized by New Hampshire until 1955 and 1962, respectively. In the meantime, Roberts had died in November 1932, and Geddes had passed away in June 1944, both of them unnoticed by the state that owed them so much.

The neglect was not for lack of trying on the part of Mrs. Mabelle Geddes Russell, only child of Edward Geddes. For many years she promoted the worthy idea that these two men deserved special honors. In her book about the Old Man, Mabelle included the following paragraphs:

In August 1955, Rudolph Elie in his column, "The Roving Eye," in the Boston Herald wrote that he had just been in Franconia Notch for another look at the Old Man. He mentioned that nowhere was there anything to commemorate the two men, Reverend Guy Roberts and Edward H. Geddes, who labored so hard to save the Profile. . . . Edward Rowe Snow, the Marine Historian who lived in Marshfield, Massachusetts became interested and took the matter up with the Massachusetts Historical League of which he is a member.

On November 12, 1955, some twenty members of the League drove

Camping in the Notch in the 1930s.

to Franconia Notch and I was invited to meet them there. They brought a framed photograph of my father, with a brief outline of the work done placed beneath the photograph, and a list of persons present on the back. I unveiled this and gave a talk to the League members on the history of the Old Man and the work done to preserve New Hampshire's first citizen. *

In the first edition of Mabelle's book, following her description of the 1955 unveiling of her father's picture, she added this wishful thought:

It is hoped that before long a bronze plaque affixed to a boulder and placed in the Profile Lake area will honor the memory of Reverend Roberts and Mr. Geddes and record their efforts in behalf of the Old Man.

It is sad that Mabelle's wish did not come true until 1962, and then only as a result of her persistent efforts. What should very appropriately have been an important part of the Old Man's birthday party in June 1955 was overlooked and left undone for seven more years.

In the meantime, Mabelle was busy. She often spoke with me about her father, and she showed me, again and again, the big scrapbook of

---

*The ceremony was held by the shore of Profile Lake. Ed.

Honors for Roberts and Geddes

Maybelle Geddes Russell at the microphone during the June, 1962 dedication ceremonies.

pictures and text of her father at work on the forehead in 1916, and of her and her father on their return trips to check his work and the condition of the parent ledges. Mabelle also talked to people of influence and gave public talks whenever she had the opportunity. The subject became a wholeheartedly worthy obsession with her.

In 1959 Mabelle published her attractive book *The Old Man of the Mountains (Past and Present Efforts to Save the Great Stone Face)*. The book contains many fine pictures and a stirring account of her father's work on the Old Man's forehead. She autographed my copy and wrote, "You know how much this means to me." She ended her book by saying, "We hope he [the Old Man] will remain so that generations yet unborn may see him. I hope and feel certain that everything will be done to keep him safe and secure."

By 1960 plans for the long-hoped-for memorial plaque were beginning to take shape. She was reassured of such activity in the following letter:

November 14, 1960

Mrs. Scott E. Russell
50 Pleasant Street
Littleton, N.H.

Dear Mrs. Russell:

Saving the Great Stone Face

Mrs. Russell and Russell B. Tobey, Director of the New Hampshire Division of Parks, unveil the memorial plaque.

Please don't feel we have forgotten you or our mutual interest in the plaque acknowledging your father's efforts in behalf of the Old Man. Our correspondence was placed in our "legislative" file awaiting elections and the organization of the legislature. So far as the time necessary to obtain the funds, either through our appropriations or through a resolution in the legislature, is about the same. Both probably would be decided toward the close of the next session. However, there is a possibility that with the resolution, which would carry an appropriation, the funds would be authorized sooner. So, I would recommend taking this course. If you know of a legislator that would be interested in sponsoring this resolution, I would be pleased to work with him to draw up the "whereases" and other information to make them of significance and hopeful of success. Otherwise, it would be my suggestion that this be referred to the chairman, whoever he may be, of the House or Senate Committee on Recreation, Resources and Development and ask him to sponsor it.

Please let me know what you would care to do and be assured of my cooperation.

Sincerely,
Russell B. Tobey
Director of Recreation

Honors for Roberts and Geddes

Former Governor and then Presidential Assistant Sherman Adams gave the keynote address with the Old Man's watchful profile beyond.

Saving the Great Stone Face

Mabelle went directly to State Representative Eda Martin, a friend of hers in Littleton. Eda was extremely interested and agreed to sponsor a resolution. When Mabelle reported to Tobey, he sent this reply on December 13.

Dear Mrs. Russell:

Thank you very much for your letter of December 6. I am sure that in talking to Representative Eda Martin, you have placed your interests in good hands.

May I suggest that she get in touch with me when convenient, and we will work up thoughts for the legislation to be considered.

Sincerely,
Russell B. Tobey

Eda Martin's resolution number 309 appeared in the journal of the House of Representatives on Thursday, January 26, 1961, and is reproduced in the appendices.

The concurrent resolution was referred to the appropriations committee.*

It was later decided that the plaque should be in honor of both men, not just Mr. Geddes, and the resolution was amended accordingly. I am sure that this was in complete agreement with Mabelle's wishes, because I always heard her speak highly of Roberts's part in the great effort to get the Old Man repaired. Although she had started out as her father's champion, she wanted full credit given to both men, and that was how it worked out.**

At last after many years, Mabelle's dream was to be realized. It had taken Guy Roberts nearly ten years to get something done for preserving the Old Man, and it had taken Mabelle even longer to get state recognition for him and for her father.

---

*The resolution authorized that a member of the House of Representatives, appointed by the speaker, a member of the Senate, appointed by its president, and a member of the public at large, be appointed by the governor and instructed to make recommendations to the General Court at its 1961 session for a suitable plaque and its installation, together with a request for funds estimated to be required. Ed.

**Subsequently Governor Wesley Powell appointed a committee of three to work with the New Hampshire Division of Parks to select a plaque and an inscription for it. The committee members were: Representative Eda C. Martin, Senator Arthur Drake, and George Noyes of Bethlehem, New Hampshire. Ed.

Honors for Roberts and Geddes

Camping at Lafayette Place, 1976 style.

The *Littleton Courier* described the event as follows:

Dedication Is Held Sunday

In an impressive ceremony held on the shore of Profile Lake in Franconia Notch Sunday afternoon, a plaque was dedicated to two men who persevered to save New Hampshire's famed Old Man of the Mountains from possibly becoming a faceless jumble of granite.

The program honored the late Reverend Guy Roberts of Whitefield and Edward H. Geddes of Quincy, Massachusetts. The memorial, recording the efforts of the two men 46 years ago to preserve the Great Stone Face, was unveiled by Mr. Geddes' daughter, Mrs. Mabelle Geddes Russell of Littleton.

In charge of Sunday's program was Representative Eda C. Martin of Littleton, who introduced the resolution adopted by the 1961 Legislature authorizing the plaque.

Invocation was by Reverend Ernest R. Drake of the First Methodist Church of Littleton. Mrs. Martin led in pledge of allegiance to the flag. A welcome was extended by Franconia Selectman Robert McLachlin, the Old Man of the Mountains being located in the Town of Franconia.

Others participating included Commissioner John F. Rowe of the New

Saving the Great Stone Face

Hampshire Department of Resources and Economic Development; Russell B. Tobey of the New Hampshire Division of Parks; Councilor Philip Robertson of North Conway, representing Governor Powell; Mrs. Beulah Snell of Lancaster, who represented Senator Arthur Drake, dedication committee member who was unable to attend; [another committee member George T. Noyes of Bethlehem, also unable to be present]; former Governor Lane Dwinell of Lebanon, who recalled President Eisenhower's visit in Franconia Notch on June 21, 1955; and Sherman Adams of Lincoln, ex-governor and Presidential Assistant to President Eisenhower. Benediction was by Mr. Drake.

I regretted being unable to attend either one of the 1955 and 1962 events. Home responsibilities kept me away in November 1955, and I was in New York in June 1962. But my thoughts were there at Profile Lake with Mabelle and the long-overdue program of recognition. I knew how grateful Mabelle was that at last these two men were given credit for their great services to New Hampshire and to the throngs of people who come annually to Franconia Notch.

Because I could not be there to share the two memorial ceremonies, I arranged for Mabelle to go with me to Profile Lake and take some pictures. It was a happy time for both of us, and I was able to get several colored slides of Mabelle holding her father's picture and turnbuckle models, with the Old Man plainly visible in the background.

Our trip was one of the last times we were together. As her health began to fail, she gradually became less active. Nevertheless, I was shocked and saddened to read the *Courier* announcement of her passing:

Mrs. Mabelle G. Russell, 76 of 50 Pleasant Street, Littleton, died Thursday, January 20, [1977] at the Littleton Hospital after a long illness.

Born in Bradford, Rhode Island, July 30, 1900, she was the daughter of Edward H. and Nellie (Carter) Geddes. The family moved to Quincy, Massachusetts, where she attended school, graduating from high school in 1920. She became a dental hygienist and worked at that profession for 25 years. . . . She was married to the late Scott E. Russell, a native of Whitefield. . . .

I had the comfort of knowing that Mabelle had realized her dream of a fitting memorial for her father and Mr. Roberts. Her contributions are a priceless link in the life story of the Old Man of the Mountain.

Honors for Roberts and Geddes

The Old Man of the Mountain
Edward Hill, date unknown
23" x 19 1/2"
Oil on canvas
Collection: Littleton Public Library

IV

Preserving
the Profile

*T*HE MAINTENANCE and preservation of the Old Man has encompassed not only the raising of funds to protect him and his forest background and not only the careful preservation of the rock formation so exposed to the freezing and thawing weather but also the protection of his environs from interstate traffic plans which would have isolated and marred his area beyond recall.

In this last part of her book, Mrs. Hancock first tells the good news about the progress made in ensuring the continued safety of the Great Stone Face itself. Then she details step by step the often discouraging but never-ending struggle to save the fragile Notch from becoming predominantly a wide, high-speed superhighway.

On each one of these issues, deep feelings were stirred and an outpouring of concerned support has been generated. This story can stand as a symbol of the fact that all things precious to us need perpetual protection if the rare beauties of this world are to be maintained.

11

CONTINUING REPAIRS
ON THE GREAT STONE FACE

GUY ROBERTS, who worked nearly ten years to get something done,
and Edward H. Geddes, who did
the first repair work in 1916, have been followed through the years by
several other brave men in their continuing efforts to save the famous
Profile.

Still concerned for the Old Man's safety, Roberts began biannual inspection trips to the top of the head in 1917 and made six trips in all. His
last climb was in 1927 only a few years before he died. On that trip he
found that visitors had removed stones from the small retaining wall built
behind the forehead boulders and had tossed them out over the face "just
for fun." To prevent further removal, a cement wall was installed. John
J. Glessner of Bethlehem paid for workmen and materials. The work,
finished on October 14, 1927, required a rich mix of Lehigh Portland cement which was donated by the W. A. Rowell Company of Lakeport.
Along with the cement, wire mesh for reinforcement, sand, equipment
and tools, and even water had to be toted up Cannon Mountain and down
one mile to the head.

Edward Geddes Says Farewell

IN 1937 new rumors circulated that the Old Man was again in danger.
This was not exactly unexpected news, for Mr. Geddes had been to the
Profile twice since 1916 and had warned that a wide crack behind the

111

A seventy-four-year-old Edward Geddes checks his measurements on his last trip to the top on July 3rd, 1937.

forehead should be carefully watched for possible future attention.

The concern came to a head when Robert Jesseman of Franconia reported his recent findings. New Hampshire and Boston papers picked up the story with such startling headlines as "Old Man of the Mountains May Lose His Head" and "Urges Inspection of Old Man to Guard Against Disintegration." The *Union Leader* stated:

Concern expressed by a Franconia man for the condition of the Old Man of the Mountains in Franconia Notch may lead to an official inspection by the State Forestry Department with view to ascertaining if any damage has been done by the forces of the weather and what can be done to reinforce the formation and guard against its disintegration.

Recognized as one of New Hampshire's chief recreational assets, the Old Man underwent an overhauling over 20 years ago when, through the efforts of Reverend Guy Roberts, they found Edward H. Geddes to make repairs on this natural phenomenon. Now it is thought that another examination should be made to see if the profile is as enduring as it appears to tourists.

The suggestion was made recently by G. Robert Jesseman, youthful Franconia selectman, who has noticed that there are crevices in the ledge that should be sealed against moisture, and that there are certain sections

Saving the Great Stone Face

that are directly connected with the profile that show signs of separating from the main ledge which should, he believes, be securely bolted in some manner.

Being of the opinion that the rugged old gentleman should undergo a thorough renovation, he interviewed John Foster, head of the State Forestry Department, who gave an attentive ear. He observed the logic of the Franconia man's argument and promised to send an expert to the region as soon as possible to survey the situation and to recommend action.

As Mabelle wrote in her book,

Mr. Foster took immediate heed and wrote to Mr. Geddes, asking if it was possible for him to come and find out what the trouble could be. Naturally, Mr. Geddes was very disturbed. Although he was now seventy-four years old — too old to be climbing mountains — he replied that he surely would investigate.

On July 3rd, 1937, Mr. Geddes, accompanied by Lyle N. Watson, assistant State Forester, C. T. Bodwell of the Society for the Protection of New Hampshire Forests, and myself, and several others, ascended the rough trail up the mountain and down to the head. It really was a rough trail all the way, for the fine trail kept to the top of the mountain had not been cared for since the Profile House was destroyed by fire.

After taking careful measurements and comparing them with his 1916 measurements, Mr. Geddes smiled reassuringly and stated, "The Old Man has not moved one sixteenth of an inch in the past 21 years." Some 20 feet back of the forehead boulder there is a large fracture in the mountain, quite wide and of considerable length. No one knows how deep it is or how dangerous it may be. Father had measured this fracture in 1916 for he knew that it was dangerous and should be carefully watched. To quote from his manuscript, "Sometime in the future the whole Profile may slide into the valley, for there is a large fracture in the mountain some 20 feet back of the head. The ice freezing in this fracture may be pushing the whole Profile a slight fraction each year." In 1937 he found it to measure the same; there had been no movement or widening in 21 years. But frost action works peculiarly. For some time no change will occur, then suddenly movement begins again. Father made permanent markings for measuring this fracture and gave his measurements to Mr. Watson so the Forestry Department could continue to watch the condition.

"It is your responsibility from now on," warned Mr. Geddes, "for I shall

Continuing Repairs

not be on the mountain again. This is my last trip." He also repeated his
warning of 1916, that the turnbuckles must be painted once a year to
preserve and continue their perfect working order.

Before the winter set in, a little additional work was done by the State.
Back of the Old Man's head near the fracture were several boulders. These
were fastened to the mountain by tie rods to be sure they remained in
the position they then occupied. Also, some small cement blocks were
inserted at intervals in the fracture to aid in watching for any widening.

In their reports of the July inspection tour, newspapers quoted Mr. Geddes as saying, "With proper care, the Old Man of the Mountains will be the same in the year 2037, a century from now!" He was happy to give the Old Man a "clean bill of health," but the 1937 event and related publicity alerted the state to giving more frequent and careful attention to the Old Man's well-being so that he *could* endure for a century, and even longer.

Further Inspections

DURING the years following the 1937 inspection tour Mr. Geddes's fears proved justified concerning the large fracture back of the Old Man's head. The never-ceasing destructive forces of nature were widening the fracture as it gradually opened up at least three quarters of an inch more.

A decade later, in 1947, the legislature passed a "Joint Resolution for Protection of the Old Man" and appropriated $25,000 for work to "protect this Great Stone Face as a recreational asset to the State."

An article by Reg Abbott appeared in the *Union Leader* of October 3, 1950, telling of a special inspection tour. Some excerpts follow:

Ever since the Recreation Division of the Forestry and Recreation
Department assumed control of the Notch, one of Director Tobey's con-
cerns has been, "How is the Profile holding up?"

You can imagine what a loss to New Hampshire it would be if the 25-ton
forehead rock should tumble over the edge, for instance.

For years Reverend Roberts made the yearly inspection himself. When
he was no longer able to do it, he asked C. T. Bodwell, Flume Reserva-
tion Manager, to assume the task. Now the Division has set itself to answer
the questions, "Is the main ledge secure? Is there danger in the crumbling

Saving the Great Stone Face

granite which surrounds the area?"

So Mr. Tobey has arranged to have Professor T. E. Myers, head of the UNH geology department, "adopt" the Old Man, check him carefully and keep a professional eye on him from now on.

The UNH expert was unable to make this trip with us, but will do so in a few days. If he values his leg muscles, perhaps it is just as well. . . .

Assistant Director John Blackwood, Division Engineer Bob Sullivan, Tram Manager Roger Peabody, Mr. Tobey and this reporter made the trip. We figured the simplest way was to ride the Tram to the summit of Cannon Mountain, and take the Appalachian Mountain Club trail down to the south ledges.

A spot on the rim trail on Cannon where the slope seems to go straight down is where the trail goes. We stepped over the edge. . . .

It was a good thing we had rubber soles on our boots. For the first 15 minutes it was down, down, down over ledges. Then we hit a col, and a short hike through a wooded area, where 200-year-old trees are only 10 feet high, so rugged are growing conditions at this altitude.

Perhaps a half mile down the mountain, the cairned trail to the Old Man leaves the main trail, goes southeast to the ledges of the mountain and slides another half mile. It is no place for goofers.

About the time we swore we couldn't drop down another step, we found the spot — 1,200 feet above Profile Lake — where the rocks form the famous Face.

The forehead stone juts out into space, apparently resting on a small ledge. But for the steel anchors, the hiker would never know where he was.

We checked the asphalt paint on the turnbuckles, peered at the cement in the ledge to see if any movement showed, took pictures of the area, and then took off downhill again, without benefit of trail.

An hour later we were rubbing sore muscles down here in the Notch.

In the fall of 1954, at the request of the state, another inspection tour was made to the top of the Profile. The examination was carried out by University of New Hampshire and State Geologist Professor T. R. Myers; UNH Geologist and Professor D. H. Chapman; and UNH Civil Engineer and Professor R. R. Skelton, guided by Austin Macaulay, head of the Franconia Notch Ski Patrol. Their study confirmed reports that the fissure that Geddes had warned about in 1937 had indeed widened by three fourths of an inch. This was alarming news, for the section of ledge that had moved weighed about 300 tons. It was high time to call for legislative help!

Continuing Repairs

The 1958 Preservation Project

THE 1955 bill authorizing the expenditure of $25,000 for repairs on the Old Man was introduced by Representative Nina Peabody of Franconia and was passed by the New Hampshire legislature in July 1957. The legislation was promptly signed by Governor Lane Dwinell, and after much consultation and planning, the state opened bids for the work on June 5, 1958. The contract was awarded to Waterproofing Engineering and Products Company, Inc., of Revere, Massachusetts.

Publicity concerning the 1958 project began early in that year. The recreation division of the New Hampshire Forestry and Recreation Department, under the instruction of Director Russell B. Tobey, prepared a "Spring Bulletin of Information." Copies were sent to the press, organizations, and individuals, over a wide area of the country.

As plans and actual work progressed, the recreation division issued several special news releases to the Associated Press and the United Press International. This gave broad coverage of the history-making events going on at Franconia Notch. The Old Man of the Mountain was being publicized anew, and in a most spectacular fashion.

From the news releases, the write-ups in the *Littleton Courier, Union Leader*, and Boston and other New England papers, and from Mabelle's book and Niels Nielsen's article "How Long Will the Old Man Last?" that appeared in the June 23, 1972, issue of the *Granite State Vacationer*, the following account of the 1958 project has been organized.*

Six state engineers and the contractor tomorrow [June 11] plan to hike to the top of the Old Man of the Mountains to complete technical procedures preparatory to the actual start of repairs to New Hampshire's Profile.

Simultaneously, John O. Morton, Commissioner of the State Public Works and Highways Department, announced that the first major work in 42 years to preserve the Great Stone Face is scheduled to start July 21.

Approved June 30 by Governor Dwinell and Council, the spectacular $9,889 weather-proofing project will be performed by Waterproofing Engineering and Products Company of Revere, Massachusetts, low bid from nine submitted. It must be completed by September 1.

Because of the ruggedness of the terrain on Cannon Mountain and Pro-

---

*It is impossible to determine the author's sources for all the paragraphs which make up this passage, although much of the information is undoubtedly attributable to the recreation division's news releases. Ed.

Saving the Great Stone Face

Above left: Don Maybury brings the Miller Airlines whirlybird in for a landing on the pad above the Old Man. In all, 50 tons of sand, cement, turnbuckles, cables and tools were airlifted for the 1958 project.

Left: Two 30" holes were drilled into the ledge on top of the Old Man's head for each of the eight U-bolts that anchored the tie rods in place. A core drill was used to minimize vibration and yield samples for analysis of rock quality.

Above: Dan Young marking and recording the granite core samples and their location on the top of the Old Man.

Continuing Repairs

Drilling to anchor a precariously perched boulder to the main ledge. A total of nineteen were secured with 1" cable.

Assembling the turnbuckles. Seven to nine feet in length, the main turnbuckle rods are 2" in diameter and have raised threads.

Saving the Great Stone Face

With the turnbuckles in place, the chore of cleaning and covering the foot-wide fissure with a canopy to prevent the effects of thaw and freeze began.

At completion of the 1958 work, Director Russell B. Tobey (center) makes a final inspection of the new canopy.

Continuing Repairs

Engineers from the New Hampshire Public Works and Highways Department involved in the 1958 project take a last look in October. The top is turnbuckled and sealed, but the south side of the Old Man's head is still exposed to the elements.

file Mountain, from which the Old Man juts out 1,200 feet above Profile Lake, the contractor plans to supply all materials to the site by helicopter.

The first major repairs to the Old Man since E. H. Geddes, a Quincy, Massachusetts quarryman, anchored the slipping forehead stone in 1916, will consist of three principal parts:

1. Anchorage of 300-ton slab of granite, part of a ledge to which the upper forehead stone is attached by Geddes' anchor irons, to the main part of Profile Mountain with metal ties.

2. Integration of the above slab with the main part of the mountain by filling* in a fissure 43 feet, 8 inches long, 7 feet deep, with cement grout under extremely low pressure.

3. Sealing other top fissures to provide a water-proof "roof" for the entire top behind the face.

*It was decided not to fill the crack but to bridge it with a waterproof canopy.

Saving the Great Stone Face

Just 14 years later Niels Nielsen seals the cracks in the south profile with an extension of the original canopy as part of the 1972 maintenance program.

Actual work did not begin June 21 as had originally been planned. The delay was due to three factors: the late arrival of special, custom-made steel rods to be used to anchor the 300-ton slab of granite to the main ledge of the mountain, additional work recommended beyond the original contract, and weather conditions that were unfavorable to airlifting the supplies.

It was on August 1 that the helicopter from Miller Airlines, Inc., of Pittsburgh, Pennsylvania, piloted by Donald Maybury, 36, of that city, began lifting materials from the Peabody Slopes parking area to a small airstrip some 500 feet back up the mountain from the Old Man's forehead. The eight-foot-square landing pad was constructed of sand bags placed at the chosen location so there would be no danger of any vibrations disturbing the Old Man. Some 50 tons of materials were airlifted in about 700 trips and 40 hours of flying time, occasionally interrupted by poor weather.

Continuing Repairs

All workers rode up and down on the Tramway and were guided by Austin Macaulay from the summit of Cannon Mountain down over more than a mile of rough terrain to the working area. Macaulay also took the photographs of all the activities.

The whole project included installation of four large turnbuckles, construction of a wire and fiberglass canopy over the large crack, building a water-diverting sluiceway behind the head, and securing several large boulders* above and around the top of the head.

Using water-cooled diamond core drills, two men from Sprague and Henwood Company of Scranton, Pennsylvania, drilled two 2½-feet-deep holes for each of the U-bolts [on each end of the turnbuckle] which held the huge tie rod assemblies in place. The water-cooled drilling caused no vibrations. Making each hole varied from 2 to 45 minutes, depending on the position of the hole and type of rock. A crew of three men poured a bonding adhesive agent into the holes to hold securely in place the huge tie rods, each of which had a breaking strength of about 75,000 pounds per square inch or about 109 tons over the entire length.

During the project, Louis Masse and an ex-Army mountain climber, Lawrence Baillargen, descended by ropes down over the Old Man's face about 20 feet. High winds made further descent too dangerous.

The weatherproofing work, originally scheduled to be completed the first of September, took nearly three months, covering 11 weeks until October 10. Within a short time the mountain and Old Man were blanketed in snow.

It is interesting to remember that not everyone was in favor of the work that was done in 1958. One newspaper remarked negatively, "The rugged profile in Franconia Notch is in danger of coming apart at the seams. If it does, it will come roaring down from the mountain in a 1200-foot landslide, and all the king's horses and all the king's men will never be able to put this Humpty Dumpty back together again." Some engineers feared the work "might trigger a sizable collapse"; others declared that efforts could, at best, "be expected to only prolong the life of the Old Man" whose destruction, they said, would "ultimately be inevitable."

But the work of 1958 was completed successfully, with promise of many more years for the Old Man, as the result of the great effort. Thousands of spectators, who used the viewing machines installed near Profile Lake, or who brought along their own binoculars, were greatly impressed with

---

*Actually nineteen boulders.

Saving the Great Stone Face

the courage and skill of the crews who labored on that high and exposed mass of ledges. The workmen looked like flies on the Old Man's forehead, and the helicopter hovered like a bird around his ancient, rocky face. It was a tremendous experience to watch, even from that great distance, the important project of those summer and autumn months.

The 1958 project proved to be an important link in an ongoing program for preserving the Great Stone Face. Many people had felt, for some time, that there should be a long-range, carefully set up and faithfully carried out working plan. The 1958 project sparked a renewed interest, and in July the governor appointed Edward B. Burwell, Jr., of Upperville, Virginia, to make a long-range study on preservation of the Old Man. Burwell, a former mining engineer and a geologist for several companies, had been geologist of the U.S. Corps of Engineers for twenty years. He was instructed to study and report (1) whether further studies of the Profile should be made, (2) its stability, and (3) what steps, if any, would be feasible to slow down deterioration and protect the Old Man. He was also to make suggestions for implementing his recommendations. His active engineering background, as well as his close dealing with many problems involving the stability of rock masses, made his opinion especially helpful and valuable in considering plans for preserving the Great Stone Face.

Cleaning up debris from the October 1959 landslide from Mount Lafayette which covered the road to the edge of Profile Lake.

Continuing Repairs

About a year later Burwell submitted his recommendations, which are reproduced in the appendices.

How these recommendations were carried out are explained in the next chapter as a new, vigorously devoted man was moving onto the scene.

Introducing Niels Nielsen

NO ONE ELSE has been so close to the Old Man for so many years as Niels F. Nielsen, Jr., of Plymouth, New Hampshire. The preservation of the Profile has been in his personal care since 1965, and for five years before that he was an important member of the inspection and repair crews.

Niels Nielsen, a bridge construction superintendent, is a big, rugged man, truly a man "to match his mountain." His devotion and courage in the annual inspection and repair activities measure up to his imposing stature. He is well known around the state for his talks on the Profile and his collection of photographs, slides, tools, specimens of granite from the Old Man, and movies by Austin Macauley who for several years has been his close companion in the work.

In Niels Nielsen's own words,

I first saw the Old Man in 1947 on a trip through Franconia Notch with my fiancé Louise Colburn of Plymouth, New Hampshire, who became my wife the next year. In the years before and after, I made several trips around the world, but I have never seen anything that compares with our Old Man. Little did I realize then, that in 1960 I would be employed by the New Hampshire Highway Department and shortly after be a member of a crew dispatched to inspect and maintain the Old Man.

On September 12, 1960, when Niels was hired by the New Hampshire Public Works and Highways Department, he was designated a bridge construction foreman. Eleven months later he was promoted to bridge construction superintendent in charge of maintenance and repair of state-owned bridges north of a line of Littleton and Franconia, and including Carroll, Hart's Location, Bartlett, Gorham, and Shelburne.

Shortly after he was hired, on September 25, Niels made his first trip with the inspection crew to the top of the Old Man. The night before, when Superintendent Adolphus Bowles of Landaff said, "Tomorrow morning we will meet at Cannon Mountain and go up to inspect the Old Man," Niels was, as he later admitted, "sure surprised." In his own account, "We met the next morning and with Sonny (Austin) Macauley leading the way; we rode the Tram to the summit and hiked to the Old Man. There we assisted Harry Sleeper and Bucky Buchanan, two highway engineers, to take strain tests on the turnbuckles that had been installed in 1958. They used an electronic device and we used a mechanical setup. It soon became apparent that for some reason we were able to get better results with our device, and in 1961 the use of the electronic setup was done away with."

In describing that early experience, Niels recalls, "That first trip to the Old Man, for this big city Brooklyn boy, was really exhilarating. I had sailed around the world several times as a merchant seaman, and I had never seen anything like him. My first impression was that he was one large, chiseled piece of rock, but when you get up there, it really is just a pile of rocks, a pile of rocks that should not be there at all! I don't believe anyone can be up there even for one trip and not feel the presence of God and be awed at the magnificence of His handiwork in taking a pile of rocks and shaping them into that great Profile."

Continuing Repairs

12

PRESERVING THE OLD MAN*

DURING the first five years I was with the New Hampshire Highway Department (1960-65) Adolphus Bowles of Landaff was in charge of the work parties assigned to care for the old Man. The guiding and arrangements for the trips up to the Profile were the responsibility of Austin Macauley, however. These were years of learning for me, and in December 1965 "Dolph" Bowles turned the project over to me.

Since that time we have taken annual strain tests on the turnbuckles and kept all the steel members rust free by painting them with an asbestos fiber-filled paint which insulates as well as protects them. We have recovered the canopy on the Old Man's forehead several times with fiberglass cloth and recoated it many times with an epoxy mixture.

In 1968 my crew consisted of my three eldest sons, Tom, Bob, and Mike, along with Austin Macauley and several men from Cannon Mountain. In 1969 my youngest son, David, then eleven years old, joined us and has been a volunteer member of every inspection work party since.

Over the years, I had become more and more concerned about the two large cracks in the south face. Even though the upper one is covered on

---

*Mrs. Hancock's original manuscript contained a chapter entitled: "The Niels Nielsen Years" in which she had planned to give a chronological account of Mr. Nielsen's work on the Old Man. She died before she could obtain much of the necessary information, and Mr. Nielsen kindly consented to contribute this chapter so that the record would be complete. Ed.

the top by a canopy installed in 1958, both were open and exposed to the winds and rain from the south. These winds would pluck dirt and granite dust from the face of the mountain and drive it into the cracks; then the rains would soak it all. The water in this large "sponge" could not drain or dry out before the cold weather would freeze it into a powerful expanding mass.

I discovered this condition in 1971 when I descended the sides to inspect the vertical positions of the Old Man from a boatswain's chair. I trusted my safety to the capable hands of foreman Doug Clark and crewmen Ray White, Art Smith, Ed Bray, Oscar Beaulieu, Andy Bergin, and son David when I spent the better part of two days examining the Profile in this way. I found the front face quite broken and crisscrossed with thin cracks. Many smaller pieces seemed to be held together like a jigsaw puzzle. Alongside and a little above the nose there is a stack of boulders. The second boulder in the stack is arched, and the outer leg of the arch that rests on the bottom boulder is not very rugged. I spent some time trying to clean out the cracks in the south face, but the tools we had proved inadequate. I was able to remove several small trees that were rooted in the debris.

In 1972 I was able to remove most of the debris in both cracks and then install a membrane of wire cloth coated with epoxy over the openings, thereby eliminating most of the frost pry danger in that area. At the same time, the stack of boulders was stabilized by chinking the arch with pieces of granite, which I then mortared in place.

In 1973 the south face membrane was recoated with epoxy to make it more watertight and durable. A number of strategic checkpoints were developed by drilling and installing pins in the vertical faces. This gave us a way of checking for any movement of individual pieces. In 1974 no change in these measurements was found.

In 1975 a good part of our time was spent in just resealing the top canopy, after vandals had cut initials right through the waterproof membrane.

In 1976 we took the strain tests, measured all checkpoints, and recoated the south face membrane, which was showing the erosive effect of the buffeting winds that blow granite dust like a never-ceasing sandblast against the Old Man. Also, we sealed small cracks in the south face and resealed others.

Since then I have followed a routine each year of going up to the Old Man in June to check his condition and deciding what must be done. Then, in July or August, David and I spend two or three days performing the

Preserving the Old Man

Top left: 1980 marked the first time two men were ever photographed working on the profile together. Below, Niels Nielsen and above, son David.

Left: Nielsen and Mickey Libby of the Cannon Mountain crew inspect two boulders loosened by heavy rain which came to rest on the Old Man's head in a mini-slide. They were removed by helicopter.

Above: Nielsen logs measurement between two of thirty check points in the vertical face. Lafayette campground and Route 3 are to the left of the chin.

Saving the Great Stone Face

View straight down from south face shows what it takes to clean out the Old Man's ear; one Nielsen on bos'n's chair and one garden hoe.

A bit later, the crew gets ready for a frontal descent; (from left) David Nielsen, Andy Bergin behind Oscar Beaulieu, Bob Welch behind Niels Nielsen, Doug Clark, Bingo Anderson, and Ed Bozy.

Preserving the Old Man

Top left: Team effort; Niels Nielsen repairs the left cheek with nine men in support.

Left: Nielsen measures check points 1400 feet above Route 3.

Above: During 1982 inspection Nielsen, standing by the mouth, and his son David, on the nose, take time out to wave to the photographer.

Saving the Great Stone Face

necessary repairs, and during recent years working over the edge in the boatswain's chair. Dave takes time off from his job in Belmont where he is a member of the police department.

More and more people are getting involved in an effort to come up with information as to how stable the Old Man really is and what can be done to ensure his continued existence.

A group from Dartmouth completed a survey and profile of the Old Man in which the report expressed a deep concern for the Old Man's "adam's apple" or "keystone" under his chin, the loss of which would probably spell doom to the Profile in 1974, due to increased cantilevered weight. I share that concern, but not the opinion that nothing can be done about restoring the keystone because it would be too dangerous to the workers. Work on the keystone under the chin would be intimidating and very dangerous, but I have given the problem much thought and believe that it can be done. None of the men who work on the Old Man does so without being in danger.

Two New Hampshire geologists have a plan for a new method study of the penetration of the ledges into the mountain. I believe that these two programs should now be considered, weighed, and funded by the New Hampshire General Court.

Recently, Department of Resources and Economic Development Commissioner George Gilman invited me to share my suggestions for accomplishing the repairs and securing of the keystone. Councilman Raymond Burton is to accompany us on our upcoming 1983 fall trip to put the Old Man to bed for the winter. Several General Court Representatives have indicated a willingness to introduce whatever bills may be necessary to effect these repairs. The amount of public pressure needed to bring about legislative action at this time is not known.

The state highway department's consultant for the I-93-Franconia Notch DEIS study, VTN Consolidated of Irvine, California, and Cambridge, Massachusetts, has also devoted extensive time to the study of problems concerning the Old Man of the Mountain.

The Old Man is not rigid, but he heaves and sighs with changes in temperature and vibrations, which are recorded in my yearly measurements. He has a little bit of space to move — not a lot — and the turnbuckles allow for that. The Old Man "walks" — one time there will be a heavier load on one side, then it will be even, then on the other side — and those giant turnbuckles act as hinges for these movements. It is not unlike the Empire State Building; if it does not move, it will break. Even the tremors which shook New England in 1981 did not damage the Pro-

Preserving the Old Man

file, and I believe it would take a good-sized tremor to damage the Old Man. Certainly if he goes, the whole side of the mountain will go too.

The condition of the Old Man continues to change, and we continue to patch him up the best we can. I believe that we are gaining in our battle with nature. The battle that we are losing is with thoughtless vandals who continue to carve initials in the semisoft membranes and destroy vital testing equipment. How anyone can — after making the arduous trip to the top of his head and being treated to the wondrous beauty seen from there — then wreak an act of vandalism on him is beyond my ken. No one can predict just when the Old Man will pass from view. He could last for centuries or a decade. An earth tremor could take him in an instant. But if the Old Man can be preserved for even one extra generation's view, then all past, present, and future efforts will have been worthwhile.

There will come a time when I am too old, too tired, or whatever to do this, and I expect that Dave will take over. I will know when that time has come because my "decision rock" will tell me. That will be the day when I no longer can step across a six-foot gap between two pointed rocks just above the Old Man. When I have to go around, that will be my last year, and then I will let Dave take over my responsibility.

Saving the Great Stone Face

13

TO BUILD OR NOT TO BUILD

IT SEEMS that for those things we hold precious the struggle to protect them is never ending. So it has been with the Old Man of the Mountain and Franconia Notch.

Secure in public ownership and maintained with extraordinary skill and care, the Old Man and his Notch seemed destined to give joy to countless thousands possibly for years ahead.

Then a new danger loomed for the quiet Notch. The post-World War II program for the building of a network of great national highways included a north-south highway through Franconia Notch!

The tremendous development of the automobile during the 1920s and 1930s led to the need for road building to meet the requirements of the new kind of major transport. Early work was on roadbed improvement and the paving of existing intracity highways. These first highways usually led directly through the villages, towns, and even the great cities.

During the 1930s major cities and even states began building beautifully landscaped parkways with limited access for use only by passenger cars. They generally provided for separate traffic in each direction with a parklike strip between them. Some of these (such as the Merritt Parkway) were built between cities, in this case between New Haven and New York City. For the early parkways, winding curves were included for added beauty, and they avoided passing through not only the center of cities but also towns and villages. Thus, they provided city dwellers with many miles of beautifully landscaped sylvan scenes.

Climber on Artist's Bluff overlooking the Notchway Motel complex, a certain casualty of the extension of I-93.

The early years of World War II demonstrated the extreme need for a highway system that would accommodate swift and heavy traffic over long distances and would make it possible for traffic to flow from one metropolitan area to another without going through the cities themselves. In 1944 an interstate defense highway systems act for the nation as a whole was passed by Congress and signed by President Roosevelt authorizing construction of a great road system, interlocking all parts of the continental United States with each other.

The major cost of road building was to be borne by the federal government. State participation, however, was required, thus necessitating that state policy be reflected in the development of a national plan. The right to eminent domain was established for the program.

By 1947 early planning for the interstate highway and defense highway system included the use of Franconia Notch as a corridor for basic north-south traffic. The proposed highway was already designated I-93.

Much of the Notch valley is narrow, extremely so where the defile passes below the Great Stone Face and around Profile Lake and again at the northern exit close to Echo Lake. Along the eastern wall in the northern section the steep shoulder of Lafayette rises precipitously and is subject to severe

Saving the Great Stone Face

slides, which over the decades have blocked and closed the road many times.

The struggle to prevent the bed of the Notch from becoming primarily a great dominating superhighway was long and hard. Opinions of conservationists clashed with those whose approach was that road building for its own sake was the sole goal.

Gradually the idea of compromise became a reality. However, the road builders' pressure has been ever present. In spite of the compromises eventually worked out, highway expansion in the Notch will be a longtime threat.

In 1957 the Clarkeson Engineering Company was engaged by the New Hampshire Department of Public Works and Highways to undertake a traffic, engineering, and construction study for the Notch route. In December 1958 the Department of Public Works and Highways released a report stating that two alternative routes to the Notch highway (Baker River and Kinsman Notch) had been considered and discarded in favor of Franconia Notch usage. Environmental organizations immediately expressed opposition to the Clarkeson Franconia Notch plan. The Society for the Protection of New Hampshire Forests and the New Hampshire chapter of the Appalachian Mountain Club assumed leadership in the opposition. Soon a new, third organization whose purpose was "Save the Old Man, Inc.," came into being. It was headed by Lindsay Fowler. Many individuals joined the drive in opposition to the state plan.

In 1959 the New Hampshire legislature authorized Franconia Notch as the location for I-93 but specified that it would be a "parkway type" of highway.

During the next seven years construction of I-93 toward the Notch was undertaken, and the stretch from Boston to North Woodstock was completed in early July 1974. A stretch from a point near which U.S. Route 3 turns east, north of the Notch to a point on the western edge of the town of Littleton, had been completed in 1960. This latter stretch was planned as the first lap of I-93 between the Notch and Vermont.

A conflict that appeared to be only a disagreement between roadbuilders and nature lovers was also a clash between important and widely differing economic interests within the state. On the one hand, the state was eager to get the maximum amount of federal road money allocated to New Hampshire as a contribution to its economy; on the other hand, a program to maximize tourist use of this beauty spot was a very important economic consideration, though this latter interest was often not articulated.

It appeared that those who believed that a great highway was required

To Build or Not to Build

through the Notch held the opinion that, if the highway were completed on each end of the Notch, it would seem to the public that of course the Notch sector must also be completed as a standard four-lane highway. This was not the reaction of those who understood the importance of this great natural wonder to the thousands who came each year to enjoy it and the Great Stone Face.

By the early 1960s public awareness of the need to preserve a limited number of unique natural environments for the nation was coming to the fore. In 1962 the Outdoor Recreation Resources Review Commission (of the U.S. Department of the Interior) designated Franconia Notch, with its Old Man of the Mountain, as one of those areas which should be singled out for special protection. The commission stated in this connection, "The scenic sites and features included in this class are limited in number and are irreplaceable.... Improvements in these areas should be held to the minimum required for public safety and the protection of the resource, and they should be planned to harmonize with the physical environment of each site. Care should be exercised to prevent overdevelopment." This selection by the Department of the Interior highlighted the national significance of the Notch and the need for its protection.

This national recognition gave new impetus for the opposition to a major highway through the Notch. In October 1965 a full-scale informal public meeting was held in Lincoln. Information was given on the thirty-mile layout of the route planned for I-93 extending between Campton and Franconia and passing through Franconia Notch. On the following January 10, 1966, the governor and council were formally petitioned by the Department of Public Works and Highways to approve construction of that thirty-mile section.

After a second public hearing held on March 30, 1966, in Lincoln and following the presentation of a geologic report on the Notch by Drs. Casagrande and Deere, the governor and council approved the Department of Public Works and Highways four-lane route alignment for I-93 through Franconia Notch.

The Casagrande and Deere report recognized that landslides were to be expected in the future from the shoulder of Mount Lafayette.

In the last fifty years, there have been eight major slides. Six of these slides crossed U.S. Rte. 3. It is readily apparent that the serenity and majesty of the Franconia Mountains can be transformed in a moment. Take a look at the landslide scars across from Profile Lake and think of the fragility of even the "everlasting mountain tops."

Saving the Great Stone Face

Various proposals for "cut and cover" structures at the points of slide danger were suggested. These proposals were eventually dropped and the planning that has proceeded in the mid-1970s put no public stress on the slide problem. This was because a scientific study of the problem had reported that, as quoted by Randall Spalding, in October 1959, . . . "there is no possible precaution that can be taken. The cost of any preventative action to protect the highway at this point from future slides is prohibitive and its effectiveness dubious. We are keeping careful watch of the situation especially during and after heavy rains.

On November 29, 1966, Paul O. Bofinger, forester of the Society for the Protection of New Hampshire Forests, sent a letter to Governor John W. King which said, in part:

The extension of Interstate 93 through Franconia Notch appears to be reaching the stage for approval by you and your Executive Council. With this in mind, I would like to repeat the suggestion made last March that there be a Franconia Notch Citizens Advisory Committee appointed to aid in the coordination of highway and recreational planning.

Members of the ad hoc Franconia Notch Committee have worked on an informal basis during the past several months with the Department of Public Works and Highways, Division of Parks, and a number of outside highway consultants. There has been an increasing level of understanding and cooperation between all concerned. We now feel that the time has come when an Advisory Committee, on a more formal basis, can work effectively and to the benefit of the State.

Franconia Notch Supervisor Harry Reed and Austin Macauley on the north shore of Echo Lake.

To Build or Not to Build

Mickey Libby points out the talus slopes under the Cannon Cliffs to federal officials studying the Notch.

The goal of the ad hoc Committee has been the preservation of the scenic beauty and recreational values of Franconia Notch. Last spring it did not appear that this goal was compatible with the extension of Interstate 93 through the Notch. Speaking now for a majority of the Committee, however, I can say that an opportunity exists whereby the recreation and highway demands may be satisfied with an intelligent and properly coordinated highway layout.

The Advisory Committee would aid in the coordination of the proposed master plan of Franconia Notch State Park and the highway planning for both Interstate 93 and Route 3.

Conversation with Russell Tobey and Robert Whitaker have indicated a sincere interest in working with such a committee. The schedule for construction of the Interstate clearly allows enough time for the Committee to study adequately the problems involved and make meaningful recommendations.

In response to public pressure from conservationists, the governor and council appointed a five-member "Citizens Advisory Committee" to ad-

Saving the Great Stone Face

vise the Department of Public Works and Highways during the planning phase in order to "retain the scenic beauty and recreational values of the area." Those serving on the committee were: Sherman Adams, Jean Hennessey, John Carter, Harry McDade, and Paul Bofinger.

At the urging of the advisory committee the Department of Public Works and Highways gained authorization from the governor and council to hire a master development planner for Franconia Notch State Park. Because of the park's national significance, a well-known consultant was selected, and in March 1967 a contract was signed with Theodore J. Wirth and Associates of Billings, Montana, for a fee of $27,000. Half of this amount was to be funded with federal land and water conservation funds.

On September 8, 1967, the Wirth master development plan was presented to the parks division of the New Hampshire Division of Resources and Economic Development. This report recommended either the Bog Pond alternative or a tunnel through Eagle Cliff and rejected the previous findings of the 1958 Clarkeson report, which had urged building a four-lane highway through the Notch.

On June 6, 1968, the Department of Public Works retained the firm of Edwards and Kelsey, Inc., to perform engineering feasibility studies. On December 16 of that same year the engineers presented their report on the highway layout and design to the governor and council, who conditionally accepted their recommendations. Four days later the Citizens Advisory Committee submitted its report to the governor and council which stated that they "were in agreement without qualifications." In their conclusions the committee members said that the Edwards and Kelsey report, with modifications, provided the best resolution of the problem, but that neither the committee nor the highways and parks officials had resolved the basic overriding conflict between the needs of through, commercial traffic and the integrity of the park. "Study should be made as to a new north-south corridor for through traffic."

This committee appeared to be extremely successful in recommending a compromise solution. It recognized both the need for transportation and the need for minimizing its impact. However, recommendations included the great expense of cut-and-cover construction and the possibility of using a tunnel to maximize the beauty of the northern end of the Notch. The state went so far as to have a model built of this plan and displayed it in Concord. The report was accepted by the governor and council on December 23, 1968, and the committee then disbanded. This excellent report encompassed a recognition of the conflicting needs and may be seen to represent a major step to the eventual compromises made in the mid-1970s.

To Build or Not to Build

University of Maryland geologist conducting seismology tests on top of the Old Man in 1969.

Upon reading the advisory committee's report, the director of parks agreed with its recommendations and took steps to determine what could be done to eliminate or minimize the factors which tempered the committee's enthusiasm for the tunnel proposal.

The following year, on February 24, 1969, the Department of Public Works and Highways informed the Division of Parks that Edwards and Kelsey had recently submitted their final report on the I-93 study and that copies had been forwarded to the Federal Bureau of Public Roads for review. When asked if copies were available for the Division of Parks, its consultant, and the Citizens Advisory Committee, a highway department official stated that copies would not be available until after the report had been accepted or otherwise cleared by the bureau. This decision to withhold copies of the report set up a new wave of consternation in the minds of conservationists, and at the same time it was learned that the highway department was currently negotiating with Edwards and Kelsey to develop a contract proposal for detailed engineering and design of the surface route location.

Next, on March 26, 1969, Theodore J. Wirth and Associates informed

Saving the Great Stone Face

Hiker on the rocks on the shoulder of Cannon Mountain above the Old Man.

the division of parks that its master plan report for the park was going to the printer immediately and would be ready for distribution on or before May 9, 1969. Their recommendations differed substantially from those of Edwards and Kelsey.

In response to what had transpired to date, the Division of Parks issued a lengthy report, excerpts from which will be found in the appendices. The report deplored using the "tight schedule" for completion of the interstate system as justification for constructing the surface route through the Notch; pointed out that this interstate could bypass the Notch just as other interstates bypassed many cities; and urged a *full* public hearing to permit the respective consultants to present their findings, answer questions, and debate the merits of their separate recommendations.

This action led to strong public and federal government repercussions, and in 1969 the U.S. Department of the Interior informed Director Tobey of a geological survey statement which noted:

In Franconia Notch the people of New Hampshire were bequeathed a natural treasure — a magic capsule of earth, green-walled, lake-mirrored,

To Build or Not to Build

tranquil and blossoming, beneath the great granite sentinel, the Old Man's Face.... The Notch is now threatened by deteriorative use and destructive interstate highway development to the point where, as a sanctuary, it may cease to exist.

That June the governor and council approved the design contract with Edwards and Kelsey for I-93 through the Notch. During the same month the Bureau of Public Roads approved the design contract also.

Then, on December 17, 1969, the Department of Public Works and Highways entered into a contract with Wright, Pierce, Barnes, and Wyman to plan, design, and prepare construction plans for relocating certain facilities at the southern end of the Notch, in preparation for the right-of-way and interchange locations selected for I-93. Plans seemed to be pressing forward with renewed urgency in spite of the growing opposition. This extraordinary pressure to bring the four-lane construction program into reality led to a federal reaction which temporarily halted the program. Then, with a suddenness that surprised both the promoters and the opponents, everything was forced to an abrupt standstill on March 2, 1970. U.S. Secretary of Transportation John Volpe indefinitely postponed the construction of I-93 through Franconia Notch!

Saving the Great Stone Face

14

THE DIE IS CAST

ALTHOUGH Secretary Volpe's decision was good news to all lovers of Franconia Notch and the Old Man, this unprecedented action led to renewal of state pressure to keep the highway program going.

Governor Walter Peterson of New Hampshire and his administration officials joined in vigorous protest against the edict, but Volpe remained firm. He based his decision on an act of Congress which bars federally financed expressways from such scenic areas when an alternate route was available. Volpe explained that I-93 could be diverted west to the Easton Valley sector and then northward to the Littleton-Vermont link. Two days after the federal action, on March 4, Governor Peterson and his council unanimously adopted a resolution requesting that Secretary Volpe immediately rescind his order. The Volpe decision held unchanged.

While both sides of the controversy were gathering their forces for renewed efforts, Franconia Notch received national recognition. The Department of the Interior, which had given special recognition to the Old Man in 1962, designated Franconia Notch in 1972 as a unique natural area. Of the 6,440-acre state park, 4,600 acres were declared a "National Natural Landmark." The following year, Franconia Notch officially became the 159th site to be included in the Registry of National Landmarks.

This 1972 action was in keeping with Secretary Volpe's remark of 1970 when he stopped construction of I-93. He then said, "This area, site of the famous Old Man of the Mountain rock formation, is one of the scenic

Looking south from Artist's Bluff across U.S. Route 3 with Echo Lake at right.

treasures of New England and valuable resource for both summer and winter visitors."

An important milestone in the program to conserve the Notch occurred when Senator Norris Cotton of New Hampshire introduced an amendment to the Federal Highway Act which permitted construction of a "parkway type highway" through the Notch, thus eliminating the necessity for standard interstate highway specifications. This provision was enacted into law on August 13, 1973. The law provided that, upon application by the governor of the state, the secretary of transportation may authorize a parkway-type highway within the limitations of necessary safety requirements; his decision must meet the needs for the protection of the environment and preserve the park-like and historic character of the Franconia Notch area adjacent to the highway.

That same month in which the law was enacted, Governor Meldrim Thomson applied to the secretary of transportation to approve construction of I-93 in accordance with the provisions of the Cotton amendment. In October, Secretary of Transportation Claude Brinegar authorized the

Saving the Great Stone Face

state of New Hampshire to conduct studies "of sufficient scope to support the findings and determinations required for completion of I-93."

Wide awareness that crucial decisions were about to be made on the controversial plan for the highway through the Notch led conservation interests to become very vocal. An important contribution was made by *Yankee* in its September 1973 article entitled "Right Through Franconia Notch (at 70 m.p.h.)" by Don Guy.

Under original plans for the interstate, the Profile would have been viewed beside or over a four-lane racetrack with cliffs on either side amplifying the roar of traffic and concentrating the exhaust fumes.... Plans for a tunnel or a "cut and cover" highway were also discussed before Volpe's decision but abandoned largely due to cost or the blasting that would have been inevitable.... The simmering issue of the highway has been revived by the Cotton Amendment ... whereby consideration would be given in the Federal Aid Highway Act to the construction of a Parkway rather than an Interstate through Franconia Notch. The Parkway concept would give priority to environmental considerations, provide turnouts and access to parking areas, ban heavy trucking, and, most important of all, by imposing lower speed limits, challenge the whole philosophy of a high-speed corridor.

Conservationists, reluctantly faced with the fact that the Notch is both a scenic attraction and a transportation link, have endorsed the Cotton proposal as the least unpalatable solution.... Franconia Notch may yet win fame as the Thermopylae of New England for embattled citizens determined to take a stand against "improving" nature with the blade of a bulldozer.... Quoting a local resident: "Regardless of the outcome of the highway through the Notch, every effort must be made to insure the uniqueness and God-given natural treasures of this beautiful section of the North Country."

As a result of the Cotton amendment, the highway department once more undertook studies to complete I-93 through the Notch. In the meantime, however, federal legislation had been passed that required more than the approval of a state's governor and council for interstate construction.

During the latter half of the 1960s national public awareness of the potential environmental problems in the development of the federal highway systems became more apparent. A series of federal laws intended to bring consideration of these problems to the fore were passed, including the following:

The Die Is Cast

1. In 1965 the Federal Land and Water Conservation Fund Act stated that if federal funds had been used to develop a park, any land that would be taken must be replaced acre for acre. Federal Bureau of Outdoor Recreation funds had been used in the development of Franconia Notch State Park, so this statement applied.

2. In 1966 the Department of Transportation Act contained a section which stated that highway construction cannot take place in a park unless (a) there is no feasible and prudent alternative to the use of such land and (b) such program includes all possible planning to minimize harm to such park.

3. In 1969 the Environmental Policy Act required that all federal agencies must prepare a detailed statement for major federal actions significantly affecting the quality of the human environment.

In response to these requirements, the Department of Public Works and Highways, in cosponsorship with the Federal Highway Administration, entered into an agreement with VTN Consolidated, Inc., on June 14, 1974, to assist in preparing an environmental impact statement for I-93 (in relationship to the White Mountains Region). VTN worked from June 1974 to November 1976 to complete such a comprehensive study.

However, on July 8, 1974, when the Littleton-Waterford section of I-93 was approved by the Department of Transportation and filed with the Council of Environmental Quality, the Appalachian Mountain Club and the Society for the Protection of New Hampshire Forests went into action. On August 6 they filed suit in a U.S. district court requesting an injunction against further work on the Littleton-Waterford section. On August 19 a preliminary injunction barring construction, issued by U.S. District Court Judge Hugh H. Bownes, halted progress on that sector of I-93. Exempted from the injunction, however, was construction of a single bridge across the Connecticut River to replace the existing bridge, which was in poor condition.

On July 31, 1974, the New Hampshire Audubon Society and the Society for the Protection of New Hampshire Forests started distributing "A Background Fact Sheet" concerning Franconia Notch and I-93. It covered the history from 1925 to 1958 when the road controversy began, and through the 1960s and into the 1970s, including Volpe's reprieve and Cotton's amendment. Then it asked, "Where Are We Today?" It answered its own question by saying, "But All Is Not Well!" and finished with the inquiry, "What Now?" That was what most conservationists were asking — *What now?*

Among the many publicity efforts of conservationists was the July 10,

Saving the Great Stone Face

1974, *New Hampshire Times,* which devoted most of that issue to spirited articles and dramatic pictures. Its front cover carried a full-page photo of the Notch, with a caption in bold letters: HELP SAVE FRANCONIA NOTCH! and this challenge in a lower corner:

During the great "Sawed or Saved?" campaign of the 1920s, thousands of Americans gave their dollars to save the Notch from the timber barons. Today the highwaymen say the existing Notch road isn't good enough. Interstate 93 is poised at the north and south gates of Franconia Notch ready to blast and bulldoze its way through the war memorial park inside. Meanwhile, a last-ditch effort is underway to save the historic mountain pass from the heavy hand of the highwaymen.

The *Christian Science Monitor,* other Boston and New England papers, and newspapers as far away as the *Clearwater Sun* of Clearwater, Florida, carried articles and pictures in the great campaign to save Franconia Notch from a big expressway. The *Littleton Courier* also kept its readers up to date on the progress of events, as did the publications of conservation groups. It had become a battle of major proportions.

At the annual meeting of the Society for the Protection of New Hampshire Forests held during November 1974, retiring U.S. Senator Norris Cotton told its members, "It would be an atrocity to have beautiful Franconia Notch filled with cement." He pointed out that it was "utterly absurd and ridiculous" to think that a four-lane divided highway could be built in

In 1979 a minor landslide deposited several large boulders on top of the Old Man which were removed by helicopter.

The Die Is Cast

The only known photo from the old tram of the new eighty-passenger tram, at left, and the twenty-six-passenger unit it replaced in 1980. At right is long-term Franconia State park Supervisor William A. Norton, who retired that same year.

the Notch. The narrowest interstate highway corridor is "between 240 and 300 feet" in width, which would be much too wide for the narrow Notch floor.

However, on July 24, 1975, a resolution presented by State Senator Laurier Lamontagne of Berlin was passed by the New Hampshire legislature. This resolution no. 6 declared:

That the Secretary of Transportation and all concerned Federal agencies be memorialized to render assistance by seeking the most expeditious federal processing of the ... draft and final EIS/4(f) Statement [for the White Mountains section of I-93] possible in order that this long, critical, and emotional and costly issue may be resolved and appropriate positive action be taken by the State of New Hampshire.

The August 25, 1976, *Littleton Courier* carried an article headed "Cleveland Urges Notch Road Compromise." In it Congressman James C. Cleveland said, in part:

Saving the Great Stone Face

Continuing vigilance: Niels Nielsen, son David, and Mickey Libby take a break on top of the forehead of the Old Man during an inspection trip in June, 1983.

The issue of what size road, if any, to be built through Franconia Notch has been the subject of intense debate for most of the last two decades. . . . The time has come for all sides to settle the issue . . . to reach a compromise which, to the extent possible, includes the legitimate interests of all concerned.

He suggested that the park road should be

a two-lane, controlled access parkway. This two-lane parkway would be rebuilt in essentially its present roadbed but up-graded to better meet the demands of present-day traffic and present-sized vehicles, and to better serve and complement the Park. Passing lanes should be added to the extent appropriate on upgrades so that through traffic will not be as hampered by sightseers and commercial vehicles. Dividers at intersections will prevent left turns. The parkway portion should have a speed limit strictly enforced of perhaps 45 miles per hour. . . . It is essential that our leaders commit themselves to a constructive and responsible approach to

The Die Is Cast

Former State Highway Commissioner John O. Morton testifying at the public hearing in Littleton on November 17, 1976.

this issue so that the situation does not again degenerate to the bitterness of previous years. The time for conflict should be over, and it is my hope that a compromise of this type will be acceptable to all parties so that we can get on with the task of providing the transportation which the North Country so badly needs in a way that respects and alleviates the sincere concern of so many conservationists, and provides a safe road for the traveling public.

On August 30, 1976, the two-year, $1.3 million study, the VTN Draft Environmental Impact/4(f) Statement was ready. The volume discussed in detail the various aspects of the problem and was of mammoth size.

In the September 1976 issue of *Involvement*, published by the Society for the Protection of New Hampshire Forests, these paragraphs concerning the Cleveland compromise proposal appeared:

Congressman James Cleveland has proposed a compromise solution to the I-93 controversy. In brief, Cleveland calls for a 2-lane parkway from

Saving the Great Stone Face

A small segment of the crowd which attended the all-day session in the Littleton National Guard armory.

a point between the Flume and Lafayette Place, past Profile Lake and the Old Man, to the vicinity of Echo Lake. The remaining highway within the Park would be a 4-lane parkway.

Society Director, Paul Bofinger, characterized the Cleveland proposal as a "positive step, which provides a framework of conciliation for review of the V.T.N. study and a final solution."

A number of important points must be clarified and resolved through the Environmental Impact Statement process including: (a) design and construction standards for 2-lane and 4-lane parkways; (b) compatibility with Park plans; (c) design details at Echo Lake; (d) recognition of existing 2-lane highways as Notch bypasses; and (e) state and federal legislative protection against further highway intrusion into the Notch.

With Cong. Cleveland clearly joining ranks with former Senator Norris Cotton and Sen. Tom McIntyre in support of a 2-lane road concept in the Notch, a major step has been taken toward a satisfactory solution.

A draft position paper issued by the White Mountain Environmental

The Die Is Cast

North to the Notch from the Tripoli Road interchange on I-93.

Committee on October 25, 1976, commented on the limitations of the VTN proposed two-lane parkway and recommended that the existing road be modified into a predominantly two-lane low-speed parkway, following the existing alignment of Route 3. Other recommendations included the location of park visitor centers at each entrance to the park, scenic shuttle services operated from the visitor centers, elimination of most left-hand turns, and reinstitution of passenger rail service to the region. Text of the position paper appears in the appendices.

The following item appeared in the November 3, 1976, *Littleton Courier*:

> *The U.S. Environmental Protection Agency has recommended a two-lane parkway as the best solution for Franconia Notch traffic problems. It's that or no road at all, said the EPA last week. The state will decide next month among several alternatives. They include the two-lane parkway, a four-lane highway, or re-routing the road around the Notch.*

Saving the Great Stone Face

On Wednesday, November 17, 1976, the National Guard armory in Littleton was the scene of a hearing which presented and discussed the alternatives for the completion of Interstate and Defense Highway 93 through the White Mountains. Plans and environmental studies were available for informal public viewing the previous Monday and Tuesday and for formal presentation at the hearing. A good-sized crowd was present, for everyone interested in the controversy had been urged to attend. Both the morning speeches and the afternoon opportunity for questions and comments were recorded for use by the highway department in formulating the final decision. Written documents postmarked by December 1 were also to be included for consideration.

The *New Hampshire Times* of November 24 carried a lengthy report on the meeting. It said, in part:

Appearances can be deceiving, but it seems as though the Battle of the Notch is finally winding down. Less than two years ago, roadbuilders and environmentalists were glaring at each other across lawyers' desks in U.S. District Court in Concord while Judge Bownes maintained decorum. Last week, the highwaymen sat back in their chairs at the Littleton Armory and listened to these same environmentalists speak of the virtues of a two-lane parkway. There was no sense of winners or losers at the public hearing. Conciliation was very much in evidence — it looks as if people have had enough fighting over the Notch.

In the *Littleton Courier* of December 28, 1977, an article stated that Federal District Court Judge Hugh Bownes had announced a week earlier that he was permitting the state highway department and the Federal Highway Administration to proceed with design work and right-of-way acquisition for the six-mile segment of I-93 from Littleton to Waterford, Vermont. This followed a joint announcement, made a few weeks earlier, by the White Mountain Environmental Committee, Governor Thomson, and Congressman James Cleveland, that New Hampshire had reached a decision to select a modified parkway design for I-93 through Franconia Notch. State Highway Commissioner Clement had hailed the November compromise as "a landmark solution to a long-standing public controversy" and welcomed Judge Bownes's recent action as the "first concrete Federal action to move the I-93/Franconia Notch controversy off dead center."

An excellent summary of the compromise solution appeared in the *Littleton Courier* on December 28 when George T. Hamilton, state director

The Die Is Cast

of parks and recreation, wrote a guest editorial. It is reprinted in the appendices.

During the same month, *Park Plan: Franconia Notch State Park*, was published, a comprehensive report prepared by the New Hampshire Division of Parks and Recreation. It included a description of the park, its operations and budget, planning considerations, and the complete "Park Plan."

The Final Environmental Impact Statement 4(f), published on August 18, 1978, presented the proposed complete parkway concept, and the legislation making the proposed two-lane parkways through Franconia Notch official was passed on April 10, 1979. Thus, after more than twenty years, the controversy appeared closed.

It is our sincere wish that the Old Man of the Mountain may be permitted good reason to gaze with approval on the great undertaking. It is vitally related to the preservation and security of his beautiful neighborhood: Franconia Notch!

Saving the Great Stone Face

Franconia Notch
Edward Hill, 1887
38" x 62"
Oil on canvas
Collection: New Hampshire Historical Society

Epilogue

THIS ACCOUNT has shown that in the history of New Hampshire, its most identifiable physical feature has continued to exist only through the efforts of some extraordinarily dedicated people. The same is true of Franconia Notch itself, and of the wildness and the natural beauty that is New Hampshire.

Just as the Society for the Protection of New Hampshire Forests appears at various points through the narrative of the Old Man, its own life has been dedicated to preserving what is special about New Hampshire. In the case of Franconia Notch, the protection effort goes back long before the interstate highway controversy. But it was that confrontation, and the decade of the 70s, that most acutely threatened the resources of Franconia Notch.

The matter of Interstate 93 posed a special problem for those who wanted to protect the Notch for the public. It was also a special case as highway projects go. From the first there were physical constraints on the road, whether the builders recognized them or not. Putting a major highway through a narrow, landslide-prone pass defied an easy solution.

Not least among the conflicts to be resolved was a disparity of views of the purpose of the highway. The coalition comprising the White Mountain Environment Committee agreed with the highway department that improvements were needed for safety and access to park facilities. We did not agree, however, that the major concern was easing the way for traffic through the Notch. Rather, the safety and comfort of people driving to the Notch and using it posed the major issue. What was needed was a road to fit the park, not a transformation for highway purposes.

More than any engineering problems, the impact of a traditional highway on the human use and natural integrity of the Notch concerned all of us who banded together in the effort. The fate of Franconia Notch State Park, in whose history the Society was so involved, went hand in hand with any highway decisions. As we had been throughout that history, the Society was interested in preserving the values of the state park — the public enjoyment of a unique and precious natural resource.

Right up to the present day and the final design of the road, the Franconia Notch highway solution has been a compromise. The fact that we have given something to win a major degree of protection for the Notch will continue to be evident as construction leads to use of the new highway. What we also won was a major financial commitment, as part of the highway funding, to improved park facilities for the public. Many millions' worth of improvements, including a bicycle path, trail improvements, better parking and landscaping, and a spanking new Flume building and information center, will enhance the experience of the Notch.

One thing the Old Man of the Mountain does not lack is friends. Right along, the Appalachian Mountain Club, the White Mountain Environment Committee, and the Notch Alternate Route Committee pursued both the legal fight and the compromise on design in the name of saving the Notch. The publication of this book is testimony to the numbers and the determination of the Notch's friends. That tenacity has seen the Old Man through many a past crisis and will do so for generations to come.

Paul O. Bofinger

Saving the Great Stone Face

Appendices

The Old Man of the Mountain

Thy home is on the Mountain's brow,
Where clouds hang thick, and tempests blow.
Unnumbered years, with silent tread,
Have passed above thy rocky head;
Whilst round these heights the beating storm
has worn, with rage, thy deathless form:
And yet thou sit'st, unmoved, alone,
Upon this ancient mountain home.
Long as these towering peaks shall stand,
So wondrous great, so nobly grand,
Serene, on high, that face of thine
Shall mock the wasting hand of time.
Whilst all that live shall pass away,
And all the tribes of earth decay.
Old Man! thy face of rock sublime,
Looks back, through years, to ancient time,
When first the forming hand divine
Reared up this rocky home of thine,
And from the lowest depth of earth
These mountain forms had their first birth;
When on these shaggy heights imprest,
Thy changeless form was doomed to rest.

Then tell me, man of silent tongue,
How first the heavens and earth begun;
If all this bright and shining frame,
With all these worlds, from nothing came;
If all these starry orbs of light,
That glitter on the robes of night,
And fill creation's vast expanse,
Began at once their mystic dance;
Or, if from mists that dimly shine,
Worlds spring to light by power divine,
'Til all the radiant fields afar
Shall beam with light of sun and star.
And tell me where, in depths profound,
The primal germs of earth were found,
Which, rising up from realms of death,
Instinct with life and vital breath,
Have formed this wondrous orb we see
Of hill and plain and waste of sea.
Where busy life, with forming power,
Unfolds itself in plant and flower,
And upward still, with widening plan,
Kindles the pulse of beast and man.
And tell me whence, from earth or heaven
That living spark to man was given,
Which shines in God's eternal day,
When all things else shall pass away.

Moody Currier

Old Man of the Mountain

Gigantic sire, unfallen still thy crest!
Primeval dweller where the wild winds rest!
Beyond the ken of mortal e'er to tell
What power sustains thee in thy rock-bound cell.

Or if, when first creation vast began,
And far the universal fiat ran,
"Let there be Light"—from chaos dark set free,
Ye rose, a monument to Deity.

Proud from yon cloud-crowned height to look henceforth
On insignificance that peoples earth,
Recalling oft the bitter draft which turns
The mind to meditate on what it learns.

Stern, passionless, no soul those looks betray;
Though kindred rocks, to sport at mortal clay—
Much as the chisel of the sculptor's art
"Plays round the head, but comes not to the heart."

Ah, who can fathom thee! Ambitious man,
Like a trained falcon in the Gallic van,
Guided and led, can never reach to thee
With all the strength of weakness—vanity!

Great as thou art, and paralleled by none,
Admired by all, still art thou drear and lone!
The moon looks down upon thine exiled height,
The stars, so cold, so glitteringly bright,

On wings of morning gladly flit away,
Yield to the sun's more genial, mighty ray;
The white waves kiss the murmuring rill—
But thy deep silence is unbroken still.

Mary Baker Eddy

Live Free!

"Live Free or Die!"
For Death is not the worst
Of human evils, nor the only grave.
Free-born am I,
And stand among the first
To break the bonds of underling and slave.

"Live Free or Die!"
No force can ever dim
This bright, immortal flame that burns in me!
I fling my cry
To Earth's remotest rim—
In life, in death, I am, forever, Free!

Frances Ann Johnson Hancock

Saving the Great Stone Face

Notch of Franconia

Notch of Franconia, lovely the chorus
Brook, tree, and bird note in ecstasy raise.
Lofty your mountain tops rising before us,
Adding their strength to the choir of praise.

Deep in your shadowed glen where you are winding
Close to high summits, lake mirrors and streams,
Beauty unequaled is free for the finding,
Chiseled in granite and fashioned for dreams.

Beautiful Valley, so nearly surrendered,
Almost exchanged for the lumbermen's gold,
We could not stand, with allegiance unrendered,
Idly allowing your trees to be sold.

Lovely Memorial, now and hereafter,
Honor the brave in your whispering breeze.
Soldier and sailor, your young, eager laughter,
Echoes, enshrined, in the choirs of trees.

Valley magnificent, no hand shall sever!
Notch of Franconia, beautiful glen,
Pride of our State, and reminder forever,
"Here in the Hills God Almighty makes Men!"

Frances Ann Johnson Hancock

Sculptor's Chips

The southern cliffs behind the Great Stone Face
Are broad and bare. Here, mighty blow on blow,
The Sculptor chiseled ledges from their place,
And let the shattered pieces fall below.

The rubble settled steeply to the line
Of heavy forests where it came to rest
In massive depths beneath the great design
Of granite features near the mountain's crest.

The bold creation of the Sculptor's art
At last was finished, high above the vale.
Long ages afterward, my searching heart
Looked up, and glimpsed much more than stone and shale.

I thought of shattered pieces of my own,
And wondered what the Sculptor's eyes might see.
Since He had done so much with mountain stone,
Perhaps He could carve beauty out of me!

Frances Ann Johnson Hancock

Poetry

Documents

Different Names for the Old Man

The Old Man is also known by other names besides the Great Stone Face. Locally we speak of him as the Profile or just as the Old Man. He is also called the Granite Profile, the Old Man of the Mountain and the Old Man of the Mountains.

The last two titles, of singular and plural forms, bring up the earnest debate regarding which is more acceptable. Personal feelings and state legislation are involved.

The committee responsible for the publication of this book has decided to use the singular form because the state legislature has used the singular, in spite of the fact that the author preferred the plural.

Mrs. Hancock wrote, "I conclude, happily, that whichever way his title is spelled, with or without the s, our Old Man at the head of Franconia Notch is undisturbed and holds to the reassuring truth that he remains uplifting and awe-inspiring regardless of what he may be called."

Gen. Martin Field's Letter and Description of the Old Man

New Fane, Vt. Nov. 22, 1827

Dear Sir — On a late excursion, which I made among the White Mountains in New Hampshire, I visited Franconia and the Profile Mountain, which has long been considered a rare phenomenon. I there procured a sketch of the mountain, which I enclose to you, and if it meets your approbation, you will please insert it in the Journal of Science, &c.

I am sir, very respectfully, yours &c.

Martin Field

General Field's description follows:

The White Mountain range passes through the easterly part of Franconia, and presents numerous elevations and sublime mountain scenery. But the greatest elevation, in that vicinity,* is Mount LaFayette, which forms the northern boundary of the Notch, so called, and is supposed to exceed four thousand feet, in height. The Profile Mountain is nigh the road leading from Franconia to Plymouth — is five miles from the lower iron works, in Franconia, and about three miles south of Mount LaFayette. The elevation of this mountain, I understand, has never been accurately ascertained, but it is generally estimated to be, at least, one thousand feet. The road passes very nigh the foot of the mountain, from which it rises abruptly, at an angle of about 80 degrees to the profile rock. The bare rock, on which the profile is delineated, is granite, and having been long exposed to the atmosphere, its color is a dark reddish brown. A side view of the projecting rock, near the peak of the mountain, in a northern direction, exhibits the profile of the human face, in which every line and feature are conspicuous. But after passing the mountain to the south, the likeness is immediately lost.

Author's Note: General Field, born in Leverett (Everett?), Massachusetts, in 1773, graduated from Williams College in 1798 and received an A.M. degree from Dartmouth in 1805, the year the Old Man was discovered. He was a lawyer in Newfane from 1800 until he retired to pursue the fascinating subjects of geology and mineralogy. He died when he was sixty and left valuable information and specimens relative to natural science in Vermont and New Hampshire. He made an early contribution to the world's knowledge of the Old Man.

*The writer should have said "range." Ed.

Saving the Great Stone Face

Legislative Act Authorizing Acquisition of Franconia Notch

Chapter 101

An Act for the Acquisition by The State of The Franconia Notch, so called, lying in the towns of Franconia and Lincoln, as a Forest Reservation and State Park.

Section 1. Governor and Council empowered to purchase land in Franconia Notch for preservation of forests and scenery.

Section 2. Condemnation proceedings authorized.

Section 3. Appropriation.

Section 4. Bond issue authorized.

Section 5. Property to be held as forest reservation and state park; management; removal of timber limited.

Section 6. Takes effect on passage.

Be it enacted by the Senate and House of Representatives in General Court convened:

Section 1. The governor with the advice of the council is hereby empowered to acquire on behalf of the state by purchase, if in their judgment they can be purchased at a fair valuation, such lands lying in Franconia and Lincoln, including all or part of the properties of the Profile and Flume Hotels Company and the wood and timber standing thereon and constituting a part of the Franconia Notch and Flume properties, so called, as the governor and council, aided by the advice of the forestry commission, may deem necessary for the preservation of the forests and scenery, and to accept deeds thereof in the name of the state.

Section 2. In case the owner or owners of any lands or wood and timber or other appurtenances to land deemed necessary by the governor and council for the purpose aforesaid shall decline to sell the same for a price deemed reasonable by the governor and council, the governor and council are hereby empowered to take and appropriate the same for the use of the state by causing a survey or location of such land and wood and timber to be prepared under their direction and filed with the secretary of state, and by applying by petition to the superior court of Grafton county in the name of the state to assess the damages occasioned by such taking. Upon such petition notice shall be given as ordered by the court, and either party shall be entitled to an assessment of damages by jury; and judgment shall be entered on the verdict of the jury, subject, however, to the right of the state, in the discretion of the governor and council, to discontinue proceedings at any time before final judgment, but upon such terms as the court may find that justice requires. On the payment of the value as finally determined, the title of the land so taken shall rest in the state. Such proceedings shall be prosecuted by the attorney-general under the direction of the governor and council.

Section 3. For the purposes of this act the sum of two hundred thousand dollars, or so much thereof as may be necessary, is hereby appropriated; and the governor and council are authorized to accept contributions for said purposes.

Section 4. To provide funds appropriated by this act, the state treasurer is hereby authorized under the direction of the governor and council to borrow said sum of two hundred thousand dollars or any portion thereof on the credit of the state; and to issue bonds or certificates of indebtedness therefor, in the name and on behalf of the state, at a rate of interest to be fixed and determined by the governor and council; such interest payable semi-annually on the first days of January and July of each year; such bonds to mature and become payable in the amounts of one twentieth thereof at the end of each year from the date of issue until the whole amount has been paid; such bonds to have interest warrants or coupons attached thereto; said coupons to be signed by the state treasurer and said bonds and coupons to be made payable at such places as the governor and council shall designate.

Section 5. All property acquired under the provisions of this act shall be held by the state for the purpose of a forest reservation and state park, and the care and management thereof shall be vested in the forestry commission, who may make contracts for such care and management with the approval of the governor and council. Such property shall at all reasonable times be open to the public under such rules and regulations as the forestry commission, with the approval of the governor and council, may prescribe. Said commission shall not cause nor permit the removal of live timber from said lands without the approval of the governor and council except for the purpose of improving the forest growth thereon; but timber not needed for forest conservation or for the preservation of the scenic beauty of said Notch may be sold therefrom with the approval of the governor and council, and the proceeds of all such sales shall be paid into the state treasury by said commission.

Section 6. This act shall take effect upon its passage.

Approved April 21, 1925

A few days later the following act was passed:

Chapter 260

Joint Resolution authorizing the governor and council to dedicate the Franconia Notch Forest Reservation and State Park as a Memorial to the Men and Women of New Hampshire who have served the Nation in times of war.

Resolved by the Senate and House of Representatives in General Court convened:

That, upon the acquisition by the state of the title to the Franconia Notch, under the terms of the Act approved April 21, 1925, the governor and council be and they hereby are authorized and directed to dedicate the forest reservation and state park contemplated by said Act as a memorial to the men and women of New Hampshire who have served the nation in times of war.

Approved April 30, 1925

Legislative Resolution Authorizing Geddes Plaque

Resolution 309

Whereas, The Profile in Franconia Notch, well-known to all New Hampshiremen as The Old Man of the Mountain, is a beloved and famous feature of our state, and

Whereas, the natural forces which created this Profile are forever working to effect its destruction, and

Whereas, the late Edward H. Geddes did recognize this danger to The Profile: and through his investigation of it, did, by native ingenuity, devise methods to preserve its stability; and by great physical endurance, carried on his back, despite his fifty years, the necessary tools and devices over miles of rough mountain terrain to the remote and precipitous site; and, with courage and skill, made installations at the risk of life and limb in the face of high altitude mountain conditions, and

Whereas, the engineering soundness and effectiveness of the devices which he installed on Profile Mountain in 1916 are today acknowledged by eminent geological engineers, who have ascertained that the ledges so secured have not moved measurably, therefore be it

Resolved that the General Court of New Hampshire does gratefully acknowledge, on behalf of the residents of this State and the untold millions who have been attracted to this natural phenomenon, a debt of gratitude to Edward H. Geddes, and approves arrangements to have this acknowledgement made known by a suitable plaque to be installed in an appropriate place in Franconia Notch; and further recommends that a museum, to be known as the Edward H. Geddes Memorial Museum, be included in plans for the future State developments in this Notch for exhibits of the devices protecting The Profile and other scientific and historical aspects of the White Mountains, and be it further

Resolved that a committee, consisting of a member of the House of Representatives

Saving the Great Stone Face

appointed by the Speaker, a member of the Honorable Senate appointed by the President, and a member of the Public at Large, be appointed by the Governor and instructed to make recommendations to the General Court at its 1961 session for a suitable plaque and the installation thereof, together with a request for such funds as may be deemed necessary to accomplish this.

Resolution 309 appeared in the *Journal of the House of Representatives*, January 26, 1961. Ed.

President Dwight Eisenhower's Speech on June 24, 1955

Governor Dwinell, Members of the New Hampshire Congressional delegation, distinguished guests, and my fellow Americans:

Only a few moments ago, I had the first opportunity of my life to look at the Old Man of the Mountains. The natural question asked me was, "What did you think of it, Mr. President?" I answered, as anyone would in polite conversation and said, "Remarkable, Wonderful. Interesting."

The real thought that crossed my mind was: "What does the Old Man of the Mountains think of us?"

He has been there through time. In his lonely vigil at the top of that mountain, let us not try to go back to what he may have been thinking through those ages before our civilization first discovered him: 1805 – 150 years ago he saw great ox carts going through these roads where now we travel in an instant. He saw the fastest means of transportation – the horse. Finally he saw stage coaches. He saw only here and there a habitation, a sparsely settled wilderness. He has seen mankind go from the sailing ship and from the horse and buggy to the jet airplane and the ability to cross the ocean in a few hours. He has seen the great sciences of radio and television come to us. He has seen every American have with his morning breakfast the day's news of the world. He has seen the great electronics industry – electric lights, telephones and telegraphy, and all the things by which we live today. All of these changes have come about.

But can you believe, as he stands up there, in infinite majesty, that he thinks it is of great concern that we travel at a rate that multiplies the speed of our forefathers?

I believe he thinks of something deeper than that. Possibly he recalls the words with which our forefathers started the greatest of all human documents: "When in the course of human events it becomes necessary for one people to dissolve the political bands which have connected them with another, and assume among the powers of the earth that separate and equal status that both the laws of nature and nature's God intended them, a decent respect for the opinions of mankind impel them to declare the reasons which have led to their separation. We hold these truths to be self-evident, that all men are created equal, that they are endowed by their Creator with certain unalienable rights. Among these are life, liberty, and the pursuit of happiness."

These immortal words must mean a great deal to the Old Man of the Mountains. He must contemplate them from time to time. I think we, with him, understand life. We know the instinct of self-preservation, and we know what living means to us, in our separate capacities, in our separate areas. We know what liberty is: the individual's right to do as we please as long as we do not infringe upon similar rights of others.

But the pursuit of happiness – he must have noted that those writers did not create this government to give us happiness. Far better they knew than to try to define for any one of us happiness, the pursuit of happiness – our liberty – each according to his own desires, to the deepest aspirations of his own soul.

Now, what have we done about it? Where do we find happiness? Possibly that is what he is wondering today.

We know certain things. We know we would like to be at peace. We do not want to send our boys off into the Armed Services to serve in foreign lands. We do not

Documents

want to dwell in fear. We do not want to contemplate the horrible things that could happen to us in a new war.

At home, we want to live comfortably. We want to be well-informed. We want to have neighbors around us that we like. But as we pursue happiness, are we thinking only of these material things? Then how do we attain it?

If we attain money to do certain things, then we want more money. If we attain a high office, we want a higher one. If there is no higher one, we would like to invent it. We always want something more.

Now, what is there more? Maybe the "more" is to try to discover what others around us find as their idea of the pursuit of happiness, what it is that mankind wants, instead of each of us separately. Can we integrate the desires, the aspirations, the hopes of our community, and then do our part to achieve that?

In so doing, I wonder whether the Old Man wouldn't approve of us more than he may at present. Because he well knows, as he has watched us, that each individual is made up of two sets of qualities. One we know, the noble: courage, readiness to sacrifice, love for our families, respect for others.

And he knows also those other qualities, of selfishness and greed and ambition, and things that set men one against the other, and nations one against the other. He recognizes the right of a group, whether it be community, or whether it be nation, to protect itself, to make use of its own security. But certainly he must applaud every effort we make to understand others, whether it be individuals, or cities, or states or nations, to understand others as we understand ourselves, and in this way bring somewhat closer, each by his own effort, that great dream of mankind: a peaceful world in which each of us may continue to develop. Whether we do it through church, or through schools, through any kind of community enterprise, through the family, through our own reading, we do not seek knowledge for itself. We do not seek acquaintanceship with the classics merely that we may quote a line from them.

We seek the knowledge and the thinking of the past that we may bring it together — here today — and help forward, each in his own little fashion, that great progress that I am certain the Old Man of the Mountains yet hopes that mankind will achieve: that objective of peace on earth, good will to men.

I would not for a moment leave this stand with the thought that we may have these things merely by thinking, or hoping, or wishing. But behind every effort there must be an aspiration, there must be a devotion to a cause. If we are sufficiently devoted to the cause of peace, to the kind of progress of which I speak, we will be strong, and then we will be able to cooperate — weakness cannot cooperate, it can only beg; we will be able to cooperate and to help lead the world toward that promised goal. So I would say our best birthday present to the Old Man of the Mountains is that we make up our minds, each in his own fashion, to do his part in bringing about that hope for mankind that the Old Man must have.

Thank you a lot. It has been a great pleasure to meet you all. Goodbye.

Author's Letter Opposing Artificial Lighting of the Old Man

34 Maple Street
Littleton, N.H.
February 25, 1955

NEW HAMPSHIRE PROFILES
Box 900
Portsmouth, New Hampshire

Dear Editors:

As a New Hampshire native, born within a few miles of the Old Man and sincerely devoted to him, I vote *NO* on the question of lighting him at night. From the first

Saving the Great Stone Face

mention of an anniversary celebration, it has been my earnest hope that the Old Man may be kept unspoiled.

People who favor the idea of night lights say that tourists going through Franconia Notch at night might have no other opportunity to see him, and that people who already have seen him might like a "different" view of him.

In reply, I point out that not many tourists drive through the Notch at night because wise travelers have learned to get over-night accommodations before dark and do their sight-seeing by daylight. Concerning the thousands of us who already have seen him, I can assure everyone he is quite dramatic enough at night, just as he is. I know, because I have seen him in the night sky many times.

I have three reasons why I am strongly opposed to any illumination of the Old Man.

1. Artificial lighting would cost money that could be used to better advantage. Two suggestions would be to restore New Hampshire's first settlement at Pannaway, and to promote the underwriting of a long-range library of small volumes about New Hampshire for use in our schools. We should be more concerned with preserving our heritage and less with outward display.

2. Spotlights would give a worldly, artificial atmosphere to a natural wonder that is sublimely spiritual in its influence. Attention would be less on the Old Man himself, and more on the lights — where they were located, how many were used, how powerful they were, who installed them, where they were controlled, and so on. Let us keep the Old Man from material considerations, publicity stunts, and fanfare.

3. The Old Man doesn't need night lighting. He can already be seen at night, and with a grandeur no spotlights could rival. In the serene silence of moonlight and starlight, or lighted only by the stars, or even on a dark night when his face is only dimly visible, it is a memorable experience to stand by Profile Lake or just stop the car beside the highway and step out. The hush and darkness make his presence more strongly felt than ever. He is a part of the centuries, not of this tiny moment; an ancient neighbor of the vast universe above him, not a plaything for little men.

By all means, use every possible modern device to keep him in repair, and let his picture appear often as a reminder of New Hampshire's welcome to all, but never impose upon his personal dignity by turning the glare of floodlights on him. Let us keep sacred the spiritual significance of this God-given Face, especially in these times when spiritual values are so greatly needed.

Sincerely,
Frances Ann Johnson

Edward Burwell's Report on the Inspection

Pierce Hall
Cambridge 38, Mass.
June 22, 1959

Mr. Russell B. Tobey
Director of Recreation
Forestry and Recreation Commission
Concord, New Hampshire
Subject: Inspection of the Profile Ledges, Franconia Notch
Dear Mr. Tobey:

The purpose of this letter-report is to summarize our impressions and to give you our recommendations concerning the Profile Ledges in Franconia Notch which we inspected on June 8, 1959, in company of yourself and members of your staff.

We met with you at Concord during the morning of June 8, and were conveyed by you to Franconia Notch. During the afternoon we rode on the cable car to the top of the mountain and from there we walked to the Ledges. After a detailed inspection

Documents

of the conditions of the top of the south side slope, we walked to a location below the Ledges from where the underside could be inspected. From there we continued to the base of the mountain. Then you conveyed us back to Concord where we reviewed in the evening with you our impressions and suggestions for further work.

Observations

We were well impressed by the quality of all work that has been carried out on the top side in an effort to prolong the life of the Profile; in particular the large tie rods, the roofing across the main fissure, and the concrete-lined diversion ditch. We found that all these installations have survived the winter in excellent condition. Only where minor fissures have been covered with an epoxy resin sealing compound, we noticed minor cracking in the nature of crazing which appears to be inevitable for such a brittle sealing material. However, where a fissure was covered experimentally with a material that remains in a plastic consistency, no cracking had developed.

We noted that on the southerly side of the ledge the main fissure and other joints are accessible to driving rain.

Our observations from the underside convinced us that any protective measures (some sort of underpinning) that could be undertaken from below, would have to be of such a scope that it would change the appearance of the Profile, would involve extremely hazardous work, and would be very costly.

Recommendations

We recommend that the following additional measures be undertaken on the top side:
1. The large tie rods should be surrounded by insulating material in order to minimize temperature changes in the rods. The surface of the insulation should be painted white or aluminum.
2. All small fissures should be sealed with a material that remains plastic.
3. The fissures on the southerly side, or face, of the Profile Ledge should be caulked in order to reduce infiltration of water from driving rains.
4. The tie rods should not be tightened for the purpose of introducing additional stresses.
5. At least once a year, a survey should be made of the length between the triangulation points.
6. Stress changes in the rods should be measured periodically.

Very truly yours,
Edward B. Burwell, Jr.
Arthur Casagrande
John Vanderwilt

Report of the Division of Parks, May 1969

Discussions to date leave the Division of Parks unconvinced that the Department of Public Works and Highways and the consulting engineers of Edwards and Kelsey, Inc. comprehend how profoundly the proposed surface route through the Profile and Echo Lakes area will destroy or diminish existing park values and eliminate or grossly reduce the opportunities for future enhancement and public enjoyment of those values which are retained under the Eagle Cliff Tunnel solution. Consequently, the Division of Parks respectfully submits that the presentation made at the December 16, 1968 "hearing" was incomplete in regard to the evaluation of the effects of the surface route upon the Profile and Echo Lakes area. The Division further respectfully submits that this "hearing" did not afford the public an opportunity to hear a full and complete explanation and to ask questions of both Departments and their respective consultants.

The Divison of Parks is gravely concerned that acceptance at the State level to locate

I-93 through the most priceless and irreplaceable portion of this park has been made without prior review and thorough analysis of its consultant's master plan report, together with his verbal presentation, and a full public hearing presentation by both State agencies and their consultants.

Recently, the Highway Department pointed to a "tight schedule" for the completion of the Interstate System. The Division of Parks can find little to justify concern for fast action when the Nation stands to lose a unique and irreplaceable park environment in the process. Surely, a day-to-day concern for a transitory "tight schedule" should not outweigh concern for other public considerations of a more long-range and lasting nature. If ever there was need to "make haste slowly," then this is the time and this is the place!

Should the surface route be constructed, we may stand forever condemned by future generations for having taken from their inheritance the right to enjoy and gain spiritual inspiration from a parkland environment which an earlier generation strove so diligently and wisely to bequeath to us, in trust that we would at least match their wisdom.

At the dedication of Franconia Notch, September 15, 1928, one of the speakers, Judge James Remick, said: "If we make this Memorial Park more and more worthy of the men and women to whom it has been here dedicated, we shall remove the last vestige of commercialism and every contrivance of man which now mars its beauty and grandeur and lessens its appeal to the soul, and ever afterward safeguard it as God made it."

It was Theodore Roosevelt who said: "There is nothing more practical in the end than the preservation of beauty, than the preservation of anything that appeals to the higher emotions of men."

More recently, President Lyndon Johnson reminded this Nation that "Beauty is not an easy thing to measure. It does not show up in the gross national product . . . or in profit and loss statements. . . . [However] it is one of the most important components of our true national income, not to be left out simply because statisticians cannot calculate its worth."

In the layout of Interstate 93, from Boston to St. Johnsbury, highway planners have worked to the limits of their imagination and engineering skills to locate this traffic *around* cities, instead of *through* them. Yet cities are transitory things, ever changing as the new eventually replaces the old. Parkland values, on the other hand, are not only everlasting by their nature, but are more difficult to restore once they have been destroyed or impaired.

If we can find justification for Interstate highways to by-pass our congested cities, surely we should find justification for them to by-pass those rare and special areas to which the city dweller so often flees in his need for refreshment.

In conclusion, the Division of Parks urges that the Governor and Council take immediate action to set aside the action of December 16, 1966, approving the "surface route with double interchange . . . for the treatment of Interstate 93 through the Franconia Notch area," and withhold further action on this subject until a presentation has been made to that body by the Parks Division and its consultant and a *full* public hearing held to permit the respective consultants of each Department to present their findings, answer questions, and debate the merits of their separate recommendations.

The Division further urges that the Federal Bureau of Outdoor Recreation, and the Federal Bureau of Public Roads take such steps as they deem appropriate, to support this appeal for a more complete public presentation of this most important issue and for a more thorough evaluation of the alternative proposals by the public officials involved.

Respectfully submitted,
Russell B. Tobey
Director of Parks

Documents

Draft Position Paper issued by the White Mountain
Environmental Committee, October 25, 1976

The key issue facing the White Mountain Region is more than getting people to and through Franconia Notch State Park. The basic issue is the preservation and management of a unique environmental and recreational resource.

Limitations of the VTN Two-Lane Parkway

The VTN so-called two-lane parkway does provide for only two lanes of roadway in the most critical area of the Notch near Profile and Echo Lakes. However, the VTN two-lane parkway is actually a 3 or 4 lane road throughout most (85-90%) of Franconia Notch State Park. While some of these capacity increases facilitate the movement of through traffic, there are more effective ways to separate visitor and through trips which do not require the type of capacity increases included in VTN's two-lane parkway. Specifically, the major limitations of the VTN two-lane parkway are:

1) An excessive amount of climbing and passing lanes creates a predominantly three- and four lane road, not a two-lane parkway.
2) The interchanges with park facilities do not minimize the need for left hand turning movements and do not represent the best way to handle park visitor traffic.
3) Other design features, including some alignment changes and the proposed operating speed, can be modified to minimize environmental damages.

A Recommended Solution

We recommend that the following solution be adopted for Route 3 in Franconia Notch.

1) Two-Lane Parkway in Franconia Notch State Park
   The existing road in Franconia Notch State Park should be modified into a predominantly two-lane, low-speed parkway which follows the existing alignment of Route 3 except at the Flume where a minor realignment creates a better environment for the visitors at that facility. Specifically:
   (a) Between the north boundary of the Park to the immediate vicinity of Lafayette Place there should be only two lanes of roadway with no passing or climbing lanes.
   (b) Between Lafayette Place and the Flume the road should be predominantly two lanes and there should be *no more* than three lanes of roadway.
   (c) Between the Flume and the south boundary of the Park the number of lanes which are appropriate will depend on the location of the visitor center and the type of visitor access provided to the Flume.
2) Park Facility Access/Traffic Management
   We recognize the need to provide convenient public access to the recreational opportunities provided by Franconia Notch State Park while at the same time maintaining the Park's unique scenic environment. Enhanced visitor access can be provided by the WMEC two-lane parkway with the following specific improvements:
   (a) Park visitor centers should be located at each entrance to Franconia Notch State Park.
   (b) Scenic Shuttle Service should be operated from the visitor centers to provide better visitor access and to improve the level of service provided to through traffic.
   (c) Park facility access during off peak periods, when use of the shuttle system is not essential, can be improved by elimination of left hand turns wherever possible.
3) Other Improvements
   Signs should be installed at the northern and southern approaches to the Park

Saving the Great Stone Face

to warn through traffic when congested conditons in the Notch do occur and to suggest use of the Route 112-116 bypass. We encourage the reinstitution of passenger rail service to the region, particularly during the recreation season in order to provide a long-distance alternative to the automobile.

Conclusion

We believe the alternative described in this paper represents a creative solution which provides improved service to through traffic and facilitates visitor access to park facilities without capacity increases.

We urge all interested groups and individuals to give this proposal serious consideration and recommend this alternative as the best solution for Franconia Notch.

Guest Editorial written by George T. Hamilton in the Littleton Courier, December 28, 1976

It has been gratifying to us in the Division of Parks and Recreation to participate with the Department of Public Works and Highways and the various conservation interests in arriving at a compromise solution to the highway controversy in Franconia Notch.

Through the initiative of Rep. James Cleveland and his administrative assistant, Bill Joslin, the diverse interests in the continuing Franconia Notch/I-93 controversy sat at the same table frequently over a period of about three months this past fall and late summer and hammered out a compromise positon with which each party felt it could live, realizing as in all compromises there were certain aspects of the proposal which were not particularly palatable to each party.

The compromise solution recently agreed upon by the Department of Public Works and Highways, the Division of Parks and Recreation, the Appalachian Mountain Club, and the Forest Society resulted in a highway proposal which will be for the most part a two-lane parkway within the park itself. For about .8 of a mile in the very southerly portion of the park in the Flume area, a four-lane divided parkway is proposed, narrowing to a two-lane undivided parkway just north of the Flume but carrying a truck passing lane for about two miles northward to the vicinity of Lafayette Place. From there to the junction of Route 18 north of Profile Lake, a two-lane undivided parkway configuration is planned, then moving to a four-lane divided parkway in the northern extremity of the park, quickly becoming a four-lane interstate roadway at the northern park entrance.

At the Flume, visitor facilities will be relocated southerly of the present location and somewhat eastward. New parking areas will be provided, along with a visitor interpretive center. . . . The Flume bus road will be maintained. . . . The bathing beach will be maintained also.

Maintenance facilities will be removed from the Tramway area with the exception of those absolutely necessary for the operation of the Tramway. They will be relocated closer to the Peabody Slopes area. The Park Plan calls for the relocation of Route 18 to the north of the large Peabody Slopes parking area, thus eliminating the safety hazard now existing which requires skiers to walk from their cars across the highway to the ski facilities.

At some time in the future if a shuttle bus system should be deemed feasible to ease traffic congestion in the Park, parking lots can be developed just north of the southern park boundary and to the east of Route 3, while there exists already, ample parking space at the Peabody Slopes area of the park.

The Division of Parks and Recreation is looking forward with much anticipation toward a resolution of the highway problem in Franconia Notch, and the establishment of a new modern Tramway [dedicated May 1980] along with a variety of park improvements which will better serve visitors to Franconia Notch State Park.

Documents

Suggested Readings

Those interested in reading further about Franconia Notch and the Old Man of the Mountain will find references to both subjects in the many histories of the Granite State but few books and pamphlets devoted exclusively to them. The following selected readings may be consulted, for the most part, in the Abbey Greenleaf Library in Franconia, Baker Library at Dartmouth College, and the New Hampshire State Library at Concord. For a more complete listing of references to these subjects, readers are referred to *New Hampshire, A Bibliography of Its History*, prepared by the Committee for a New England Bibliography, which was published in 1979 by G.K. Hall & Co. of Boston, and is presently being reissued by the University Press of New England.

Anderson, Leon Wilhelm, *Old Man of the Mountain. Born: in the creation. Resides: in Franconia Notch.* Concord, Evans Printing, 1970, Pp. [21].

Bruns, Paul Eric, *A New Hampshire everlasting and unfallen: an illustrated history of the Society for the Protection of New Hampshire Forests.* (Concord), Society for the Protection of New Hampshire Forests, 1969, Pp. 95.

Burrows, Fredrika, "The Agony of the Old Man of the Mountains." *NH Profiles*, 23 (June, 1974), 66-69.

Crouch, H. Bentley, "Narrow gauge to the notch." *B & M Bulletin*, 7, (Summer, 1976), 19-31. (Profile & Franconia Notch Railroad.)

"Fight for Franconia" *NH Profiles*, 1 (May, 1952), 16-18, 52-53. (The 1923-1928 struggle to save the Notch from lumbering interests.)

Greenleaf, Charles Henry, *History of the Old Man of the Mountain, the Flume, 1857-1931.* Boston, F. B. Moulton [1931], Pp. [17].

Guy, Don, "Right through Franconia Notch." *Yankee*, 37 (Sept. 1973), 64-69, 182-186. (Old Man of the Mountain.)

Hawthorne, Nathaniel. *The Great Stone Face and other tales of the White Mountains.* Boston, Houghton Mifflin Co., 1882. (Many earlier and later printings. Written in 1845.)

Johnson, Frances Ann, *Do You Know New Hampshire?* Littleton, Courier Printing Co., 1951, Pp. 56.

----- *Introduction to New Hampshire.* Concord, Sugar Ball Pr., 1951, Pp. 235.

----- *The Old Man of the Mountains.* (New Hampshire Pocket Series No. 1.) Littleton, Courier Printing Co., 1953, Pp. 16.

Roberts, Guy, *The Profile, and how it was saved: a brief story giving the facts about the Profile in Franconia Notch in New Hampshire.* Ist. ed., Littleton, Courier Printing Co., (1917), Pp. 22; 8th ed., Whitefield, 1928, Pp. 31.

Russell, Mabelle Geddes, *The Old Man of the Mountains: past and present efforts to save the Great Stone Face.* State of New Hampshire Recreation Division, Littleton, Courier Printing Co., 1959, Pp. 24.

Welch, Sarah N. (Brooks), *Franconia Notch: history and guide.* [Littleton, Courier Printing Co.], 1959, Pp. 32.

Illustrations and Credits

In selecting illustration for *Saving the Great Stone Face* well over a thousand photographs, stereographs, paintings, engravings, and memorabilia relating to the Old Man and the Notch were reviewed. Those finally selected came from four principal sources: the collections and archives of the New Hampshire Historical Society; the Geddes photo collection of the Littleton Area Historical Society; the private collection of Richard F. Hamilton, Executive Vice President of White Mountains Attractions Assoc.; and the collection of Austin Macauley, presently Mountain Manager at Loon Mountain Recreational Area. To them, and to all others who helped by providing photographs of specific subjects and events, the editor and publisher are deeply grateful.

In the following, all illustrations are listed chronologically as they appear in the book. The abbreviated title of each is followed by the source and/or photographer or delineator's name where known, and the page number on which the illustration appears. The New Hampshire Historical Society is abbreviated NHHS, and the Littleton Area Historical Society LAHS.

Illustrations and Credits

Index

Index

In Appreciation

The Franconia Area Heritage Council extends warm appreciation to those who purchased the specially bound and numbered edition of this book, and in so doing helped to make possible publication at this time. The names of those who participated are listed alphabetically below.

Sherman Adams
Lucy McKean Aldrich —
  In Memory of Harry J. Aldrich
Mrs. John S. Ames, Jr.
Elizabeth L. Anderson —
  In Memory of Lawrence Gilman
Harriet Hollister Andrews —
  In Memory of Clay Harvey Hollister, Jr.
Appalachian Mountain Club
Abigail Avery
Mr. & Mrs. C. J. Ayer
C. Benjamin Bailey —
  In Memory of C. Parker Bailey
Gage Bailey
Carol Stoll Baker —
  In Memory of Gerald Stoll
Miss Barbara D. Barrand
John K. & Zdenka K. Bartz
Mildred A. Beach
Mr. & Mrs. John H. Beardsley
Bonnie Beaubien
Mr. & Mrs. Richard E. Bennink
Herbert E. Bixler
C. H. Blake, Jr.
John T. Bottomley
Robert P. Burroughs
Mr. George H. Burroughs III
Donald H. Burton
Walter & Grace Burton —
  In Memory of Robert F. &
  Maude B. Gallagher
Mrs. Roland P. Carreker, Jr.
John P. H. Chandler, Jr.
Eleanor Childs
Chocorua Forestlands Ltd. Partnership
The Rev. Roger Pecke Cleveland
Peg Colburn
Mr. & Mrs. Alden D. Colby
Elizabeth Pope Compton —
  In Memory of Winifred Ayers Tunell
  Pope

Mr. & Mrs. Joseph N. Connors
Letty Elise Crosby
Mr. & Mrs. G. Huntington Damon
Elizabeth R. Dana
Dolores DeP. Daniels
Charles F. Doe
Ralph A. Downs, M.D.
Granton H. Dowse
Dudley-Tucker Library —
  In Memory of Helen M. Reed
Denley W. Emerson —
  In Memory of Dudley Richards Emerson
Richard L. Emerson, C.L.U.
Bruce & Joanne Engler
Warren H. Falls
Mr. & Mrs. Merrill P. Fay
Mrs. Merrill P. Fay
Anthony Ferrelli
Hamilton Ford
Mrs. Robert D. Forgan
Franconia Area Heritage Council
Tom & Lil Gage —
  In Memory of Stephen Thomas Gage
Richard Gallant
Jane F. Garry
Charles M. Geilich
Suzanne B. Gillis
Mr. & Mrs. William H. Gilmore and sons
Ruth Ayres Givens —
  In Memory of Philip W. & Alice T. Ayres
Mrs. Ernst Glaessel
Walter & Eleanor Goddard
Peter P. Hale
Eunice K. Halfmann —
  In Memory of Pearl J. &
  Earl W. Whittemore
Dick Hamilton
Mrs. Mead Hartwell —
  In Memory of Mead Hartwell
Mr. & Mrs. Bernard Hall Herbert
  & family
Howard H. & Patricia J. Hill
Mrs. Douglas Horton
Richard R. Hough

Saving the Great Stone Face

Beatrice M. Hunt
Indian Head Bank North
Laura G. Jacques
Mrs. Ruth H. Johnson —
    In Memory of Frances Ann Johnson
    Hancock
Mr. & Mrs. William E. Keach —
    In Memory of G. Robert Jesseman &
    Alice B. Jesseman
Karl Kelley
Warren F. Kimball, Jr.
Mr. & Mrs. B. Leonard Krause
Professor & Mrs. Peter Kyle
Langdon Library
Sophie P. Lehar
Daniel F. Lord —
    In Memory of Vivian Sutherland Lord
Mr. & Mrs. John H. Lyman
Stuart & Evangeline Machlin
Mr. & Mrs. Allen K. MacNeil
Mrs. John W. Masland
Mr. Thomas N. Masland
Miss Katharine Matthies
Willy E. Mayer
Mr. & Mrs. James P. Mayo, Jr.
Mr. & Mrs. George E. McAvoy
Paul & Linda McGoldrick
Raymond E. Moore
Mrs. E. W. Morehouse
James A. Moulton
Mt. Washington Management Co., Inc. —
    In Memory of David Drummond
New Hampshire Federation of Women's
    Clubs
David & Janet Nixon
North Country Council, Inc.
Eleanor C. Parker —
    In Memory of Leander F. Parker
Robert B. Parkhurst
Norman & Betty Paul
Charles Penrose, Jr.
John Pepper
Douglas A. Philbrook
Greta Poulsen
Profile Bank, FSB
Mr. & Mrs. Wilford J. Rand
The Rev. & Mrs. William E. Rasche
Mr. & Mrs. Carroll P. Reed
Robert C. Rooke

Edwin & Janet Hancock Rudin
James Saturley
Mr. Karl Schaffer
Laura R. Sherman —
    In Memory of C. T. Bodwell &
    Merle C. Sherman
Mr. & Mrs. Bailey B. Simmons
Norm & Shirl Sivin
Eric Parkman Smith
George & Florence Smith
Society for Protection of N.H. Forests
Mr. & Mrs. Charles A. Spaulding
Sport Thoma, Inc.
Philip Ellis Stevens
Mr. & Mrs. John Stevenson
Mrs. Gilbert T. Steward
Francis J. Sullivan, Jr.
Douglas M. Swett
Catherine B. Symmes
Ignaz F. & Brigitte Szakmary
Mr. & Mrs. Gaylord E. Taylor, Sr. —
    In Memory of Silas Lovell Taylor
John K. & Ruth C. Taylor
Dr. & Mrs. Warren Justin Taylor
Arthur A. Tilton —
    In Memory of Etta M. Tilton
Jack & Midge Tilton
Helen B. Tomb
Mr. & Mrs. William E. Tucker, Jr.
University of New Hampshire Library
Paul & Paula Valar & daughters
Mr. & Mrs. Richard G. Verney
William H. Weatherbee
Sarah N. Welch —
    In Memory of Luke Brooks, Old Man
    Discoverer
W. T. Welsh
J. H. Wetenhall
White Mountain Lumber Company —
    In Memory of Emmet J. Kelley
White Mountains Attractions Association
Mr. & Mrs. Edward J. Woods
Karl Yost —
    In Memory of Laverna Imes Yost

In Appreciation

Saving
the Great
Stone Face

has been published
in a limited first edition
of two thousand copies,
of which
one hundred and sixty
have been specially bound
and numbered.
This is copy number